Marketing Communications in English

Erica J. Williams

WAYZGOOSE PRESS

Marketing Communications in English

Copyright © 2016 by Erica J. Williams
Published by Wayzgoose Press.

Edited by Dorothy E. Zemach.
Cover design and interior formatting by DJ Rogers.

ISBN-10: 1-938757-27-0
ISBN-13: 978-1-938757-27-3

ACKNOWLEDGMENTS

I would like to thank the following for their valuable feedback and support:

Grey Düsseldorf GmbH, Germany: Particularly Mona Elobeid for her contribution to Chapter 2 (Campaign Management); Angelika Frye, Art Director at Grey Shopper, for her contribution to Chapter 4 (Promotion); Franziska Klockner, Svenja Lutter, Esther Miguletz, Julian Holland-Moritz and Julia Weidemann, advertising trainees; and everyone in the digital unit.

Hochschule Düsseldorf (University of Applied Sciences), Germany: All my past and present students of B.A. Communication and Media.

Vicki Hollett who encouraged me to go ahead with this project.

My editor, Dorothy Zemach, for her professional and friendly approach and her contribution to the final version of this work.

Table of Contents

Marketing Communications in English

Why?

Marketing Communications and the English language are inextricably linked in the onward march towards globalisation. Consumer attitudes towards brands, technologies and the use of products are evolving and the industry is consolidating. Global brands have strong consistent brand cultures, which call for unified and cohesive marketing approaches. English is the underpin of these changes so that anyone involved in marketing communications today needs to be able to work wholly or partially in English. This book is thus all about creating, designing and implementing marketing communications in English.

Who?

Marketing Communications in English is designed for students in university courses or those working in agencies, in-house agencies, corporate communications and/or marketing departments who do not have English as a native language, need to learn specialist vocabulary and practise completing work-related tasks in English.

What?

Each chapter introduces theory and the specialist vocabulary of marketing communications with thought provoking case study texts exploring topic areas and consolidating specialist terms. The case of 'Domos', a fictional global player in household cleaners, soaps, and detergents and its brands such as 'CleanIT!' and 'Bright White', is told throughout, so that tasks, exercises, and role plays for the client Domos can be completed. Tasks mirror what happens in the workplace leading from interpretation of the client briefing through to developing a new corporate identity to creating communications strategy for an international brand. Role plays include meetings, negotiations, and pitch presentations specific to the marketing communications industry. There is an additional word bank at the end of each chapter, so that further professional expressions can be learnt.

How?

Marketing Communications in English is designed for use in university and vocational study courses or in in-company and in-agency training schemes working with a lecturer, teacher or trainer who can give comprehensive feedback. Self-study or reference work is also possible as a full answer key is given at the back of the book. Users are advised to use complementary materials covering English grammar, meetings in English, negotiations in English, and presentations in English.

1 BRANDING

Introduction

Branding summons up a unique character for a product or service in the minds of consumers and encourages purchase of that product or service. It thus supports and determines the effectiveness of marketing communications activities. Companies and organisations seek to create positive and consistent ideas, images, and feelings connected to the product or service to generate trust and loyalty and to reflect the experience that consumers have with the product or service. Brands are valuable intangible assets.

Discuss:

- Which computer technology brands do you recall?
- Which washing powder brands do you recall?
- Which drink brands do you recall?
- What is the 'unique character' of each of these brands?
- Why is each of these brands a 'valuable intangible asset'?

A Vocabulary

1. Match the expressions (1-10) with their descriptions (a-j).

1. brand repositioning
2. brand personality
3. brand equity
4. brand loyalty
5. brand leader

6. brand experience
7. brand awareness
8. brand promise
9. brand extension
10. brand identity

____ a. The Fiona Starr clothing label is fashionable and high quality. The person who wears it feels like a million dollars and a person who stands out from the crowd.

____ b. Strongarm is known for its "arm" symbol, the distinctive shape of its bottle, its logo and typeface, its gold colour, and the *Strength is Within!* slogan.

____ c. You only have to see the famous triangle *PFC* logo to instantly understand and know everything behind the brand.

____ d. Penguin Airlines are safe and comfortable.

____ e. The original Vivon brand was a high quality face cream. The Vivon branding is now used on a range of products in the cosmetics category.

____ f. The true value of the GMW company was wrapped up in the GMW brand, and there was a disparity between this true value and the asset value. This could be called 'goodwill', and Master Motors paid for this when it acquired the company.

____ g. Blue Cow energy drinks were responsible for organising and sponsoring the London B6 Race to Victory.

____ h. The *Cleaner than Clean* slogan was dropped for the CleanIT! brand and replaced with *Tradition Back Home*. This new claim was rooted in feelings of being proud of a sparkling home.

____ i. Giant Burger is number one in the category in terms of branding, and it appeared in the world's top ten brands for the first time last year.

____ j. At the supermarket, I go to the shelves with all the cleaners and search for CleanIT!, which is the brand I always buy.

B Branding: Definition

1. Read this definition of branding:

> **Branding**: Blending concrete and emotional characteristics associated with a product or service and differentiating that product or service from the competition.

2. Work with a partner and answer these questions:

a. What do "concrete" and "emotional" mean in this definition?

b. Categorise the following as concrete characteristics or emotional characteristics and write the terms in the correct column in the chart:

promise, image, name, the "soul", logo, personality, connection, graphics, memories, essential truth, packaging, the "essence", symbols, a mental picture, culture, colours, (strong, positive) associations, sounds, design, mission statement, the "story", perception

concrete	emotional

3. Discuss these questions with a partner or group.

a. Would you add to or change the definition and/or the emotional and concrete characteristics of branding?

b. What are some challenges that exist for brands, in your opinion?

c. Choose a well-known brand for each of these categories:

- cars
- white goods (major domestic appliances such as refrigerators, washing machines and dishwashers used for household tasks)
- FMCG (Fast Moving Consumer Goods - non-durable goods that have a short shelf life such as cleaning products, soft drinks, chocolates and other consumables)
- TV (service or product)
- online (service or product)

4. Define both the concrete and the emotional characteristics associated with each of the products/services you chose in 3c. Use the vocabulary in the chart and your own ideas.

Useful Words and Expressions		
nouns	**adjectives**	
engineering enjoyment joy refreshment reliability technology zeitgeist	classic comfortable conservative cosmopolitan friendly funky inspiring personalised progressive quirky seductive sexy	sophisticated state of the art stimulating streamlined sturdy subtle thirst-quenching timeless unpretentious upmarket / downmarket urban user-friendly

Examples:
- **Engineering** is both a concrete and emotional characteristic used for many brands coming from Germany.
- The Fiona Starr clothing label has succeeded in capturing the **zeitgeist**.
- Vivon's branding is **quirky**, **funky** and **cosmopolitan**.

5. For each of the products/services you chose in 3c, define what differentiates each product/ service from the competition:

- car:
- white goods:
- FMCG:
- TV:
- online product/service:

C Brand Promise & Brand Identity

1. Read the definitions:

> **Brand promise**: Benefits, experiences and/or promises associated with a brand e.g. *safety* and *comfort* in "Penguin Airlines are safe and comfortable."

> **Brand identity:** Features that make a brand recognsable; e.g. the name, symbols, colours, shapes, logo, typeface, graphic features and slogan in "Strongarm is known for its 'arm' symbol, the distinctive shape of its bottle, its logo and typeface, its gold colour, and the *Strength is Within!* slogan."

2. Choose a well-known brand in each of the following categories. Then present each brand orally in terms of brand promise and brand identity:

- fast-food restaurants
- drinks
- airlines
- sportswear
- coffee bars
- washing powders

D Brand Management

1. Read this job advertisement:

Brand Manager At Domos

This is an exciting opportunity to join one of the largest and most successful worldwide FMCG companies as Brand Manager. Domos has an unbeatable portfolio of best selling household cleaners, soaps and detergents. You will work alongside other marketing professionals and join a company that offers unmatched career development opportunities.

Responsibilities include:
- bringing new products to market
- being responsible for innovation and new product development
- defining the current and future roles of specified brands in the brand portfolio
- delivering marketing and communication plans
- monitoring brand performance
- supporting activities to achieve maximum profit.

You should be results-driven, motivated, and able to thrive in a fast-paced working environment. Experience in an FMCG industry is desirable. If you are interested in this position and match our requirements, email Ned J. Smith in Human Resources directly at ned@domos.co.uk.

2. As a group, brainstorm the possible functions of a brand manager using this job advertisement as a basis.

3. Discuss the following ideas:
- A successful brand must be of good quality.
- Consumers want variety and act spontaneously. They tend to impulse buy and brand loyalty does not exist today.
- No brand is completely safe and companies have to take constant action in order to keep a successful brand.

E Branding – Case Study

1. Read the CleanIT! branding case study below. As you read, find words or expressions that mean:
- a. own brand (paragraph 1)
- b. new players on the market (paragraph 2)

c. adding to a brand with new products in the same category (paragraph 2)
d. differentiating (paragraph 3)
e. to capture the essence of a brand in the mind of the target audience (paragraph 6)
f. a brand with a story to tell (paragraph 6)
g. a person who represents a brand (paragraph 7)
h. to launch the same campaign in different markets (paragraph 8)
i. to show publicly for the first time (paragraph 8)
j. to broadcast (paragraph 8)

CleanIT!

---

(1) The total market in the UK for household cleaners currently has a value of approximately £5 billion, with four powerful and renowned brands with sizeable marketing budgets dominating the market and competing for market share. Competition also comes from both a number of supermarket private labels and smaller brands.

(2) Growth in the category has been driven by environmentally friendly cleaners in recent years. These were worth about £10 million ten years ago and have shot up by around 500% since that time. The market for green cleaners is continuing to rise rapidly with both brand extensions and new entrants. This represents both a challenge and an opportunity for CleanIT!, one of the major players in the household cleaners market since the 1930s.

(3) A small retailer in the British city of Birmingham originally developed CleanIT! in the 1900s. At that time, Birmingham was a filthy, industrial city in which house-proud housewives found it difficult to keep their homes spick and span. Harold Leadbetter spotted the need for an inexpensive all-purpose effective cleaner and started to develop different experimental products in the backyard of his shop, which his wife tried out. Eventually, Harold hit on the right formula, and he started selling CleanIT! in its original packaging of a simple transparent glass bottle with a distinctive dark yellow label. Sales took off immediately, and the product quickly gained a local reputation, with housewives from all over the city demanding the product.

(4) In 1933 the brand was bought by the company Domos and subsequently distributed nationwide, becoming well known across the country as a trusted household name. In the post-war years, sales continued to soar. CleanIT! started advertising nationally in the 1950s. The result was classic advertising typical of that era, depicting stay-at-home mums taking pride in homes that were Cleaner than Clean due to the trusted strength of CleanIT!

(5) However, by the 1990s sales of CleanIT! had begun to decline steadily, due to a number of factors. Firstly, there was a decreasing role for CleanIT! in people's lives, as Britain began to rely less on heavy industry. In addition, legislation was introduced that meant smokeless fuels had to be used in private households. In short, Britain's towns and cities became much cleaner. Furthermore, women began to spend less time in the home, and the number of single households surged significantly. Consumers stated in research that they did not see the necessity of daily cleaning and that cleaning was not necessarily women's work.

(6) As a result, Domos made the decision to reposition the CleanIT! brand. The *Cleaner than Clean* slogan was dropped and replaced with *Tradition Back Home*. The emphasis was on being a heritage brand, and the repositioning was rooted in feelings of being proud of a sparkling home. This initial repositioning was not a great success, though, as research showed it was still older women who continued to purchase CleanIT! and not the intended new, younger target market of both genders.

(7) At the turn of the century, Domos relaunched *CleanIT!* with a new formula and refreshed the brand identity. Mentions of *Tradition* were removed. The slogan became *CleanIT! for a Clean World*, and the packaging was replaced with a green bottle made of recyclable materials with a sunshine yellow label displaying the brand name in a modern typeface. Moreover, the famous talk show host Paula Mcinfrey became a spokesperson for the brand, to emphasise that the brand was for busy, savvy, and caring people who didn't want to spend their time cleaning but nevertheless needed an efficient but environmentally friendly cleaning solution.

(8) CleanIT! unveiled a new nationwide campaign at the beginning of this year that introduced a new slogan, *Power to the Planet.* The TV commercial was first aired in Scotland, then rolled out to the rest of the United Kingdom and then to other European markets. It was supported by outdoor (billboards), press, in-store and digital promotions. The campaign also introduced the character, *Mr Super Clean,* to the market.

Although CleanIT!'s image has changed over the years, it has cemented its position as a trusted brand with a rich heritage. At the same time, it manages to be bold and dynamic by being an innovator in its field. Consumers state that they feel warmth towards the brand, which is not characteristic of the category.

2. Work in small groups. In your own words write a summary of:

    a. the positioning of the CleanIT! brand in the 1950s.

    b. the repositioning of the brand in the 1990s and reasons for the lack of success with this repositioning.

    c. repositioning in the 21st century.

Presentation

1. Choose a brand and research its:

- features and benefits
- positioning and repositioning (think about demographics, lifestyle, geography, competition, price, quality, strengths etc.)
- identity
- personality

2. Give a 5-minute presentation of your findings.

TIP: Features And Benefits

Features are factual statements about the attributes of a product or service. For example: "New Xtreme washing liquid from Domos has a new concentrated mild formula for washing fabrics in the washing machine at all temperatures. The formula does not contain bleach or cleaning enzymes. It comes in 1 litre, 1.5 litre and 2 litre sizes with a new pack design. The pack is fully recyclable. An innovative feature is the X Stain Doser for accurate dosing."

Features often provide the benefits which answer the question "What's in it for me?". **Benefits** describe the solutions so that the customer can visualise him or herself using the product or service. For example: "Xtreme washing liquid is perfect for those with sensitive skin as Xtreme will not dry the skin or cause itchiness. Even delicate fabrics can be put in the washing machine saving time on hand washing. There is no need to buy different washing powders for different fabrics and temperatures meaning Xtreme is both convenient and economical. The X Stain Doser saves additional money. Using this product causes no damage to the environment."

F Brand Strategy and Brand Storytelling

1. Discuss these questions:

- Why do people love listening to stories?
- How can a brand story be told to the consumer?
- What is the basis of a good brand story?
- What can a good brand story do for a brand?

2. Complete these possible brand stories:

"I remember when I was boy/girl seeing my hero ..."
"A 'Bucket List' is a list of achievements that a person hopes to accomplish in his or her lifetime. ..."
"The founder of the company ..."
"This brand stands for adventure and this is exemplified by the story of ..."
"Our core value is the ethical sourcing of products ..."

3. Name a brand that exists on the market today that has a good story. Analyse the elements that make the brand story good.

4. As self-study or homework, create a brand story for one of these Domos brands:

- "Sunrise" – a washing up liquid
- "Magic Soft" – a fabric softener
- "Sparkkee" – a window cleaning product

5. Read the definition of a pitch presentation:

Pitch Presentation: A pitch presentation is essentially a sales presentation in which the presenter convinces or persuades the audience to 'buy'. There are many kinds of pitch presentation to sell a product, a service, a concept, an idea, a business plan, a company or a person as part of a job interview for example. In advertising, pitching can be considered a backbone to the business as it a standard business process used by clients to competitively select an agency.

Now pitch your story to your client, Domos, using this structure:

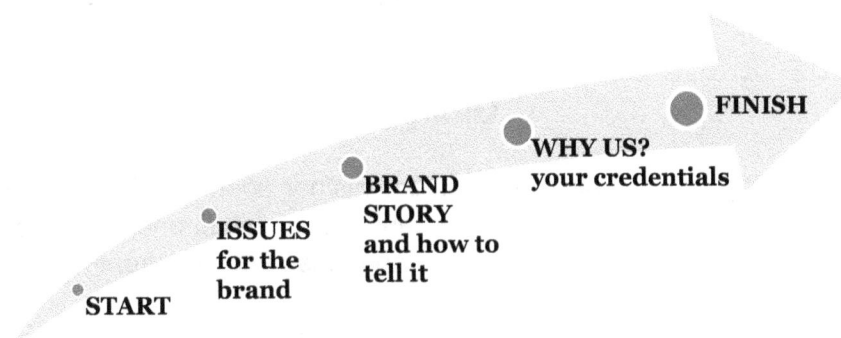

START → ISSUES for the brand → BRAND STORY and how to tell it → WHY US? your credentials → FINISH

PITCHING TIP

Demonstrate that you understand the client and the client's problems and/or issues. After this, present your solution as *the* correct solution to the problems/issues you have outlined. Then, once you have convinced the client that you have both understood the issues and have the right solution, present yourself and your credentials giving evidence that you are the right person/company /agency for the job.

Use this checklist for your presentation's structure:

_____1 Introduction: Some words about you and your background, the topic of your presentation with possible reasons why and an outline of the upcoming structure of the pitch.

_____2 A description of the client's brand and your understanding of the problems Domos has with the current branding.

_____3 Your solution to the problems: The new brand story with details on media implementation.

_____4 You and your credentials: Why you are the best person/people for the job.

_____5 Finish: Signal the end of the pitch, summary, and a strong take-home message for the client.

G Negotiation Role Play

1. Define the characteristics of an effective brand spokesperson.

2. Divide into two teams, Group 1 and Group 2. In your team, prepare the negotiation considering your best possible outcome(s), possible areas of compromise, and the interests of building a long-term business relationship.

Group 1

You represent an agency. Your client Domos is going to introduce a new range of Health and Wellness soaps called "LUST FOR LIFE". This range will have a young active funky global image and Domos wish to market the range in Europe as a first step.

You have set up a meeting with a major sports personality and his/her manager and/or agent to discuss a pan-European brand spokesperson endorsement contract. The sports personality is a basketball player whose mother is German and father is French who made his/her early career in the British basketball league. S/he speaks three languages and is currently playing in the American NBA. You feel s/he represents the young international go-ahead image Domos wants to project. Moreover, s/he is well-known and loved in the countries where Domos wish to roll out the product range. You know s/he has offers from other companies.

Group 2

You represent a basketball sports personality and/or his/her agent and/or manager. This famous basketball sports personality has a German mother and French father and made his/her early career in the British basketball league. S/he speaks three languages and is currently playing in the American NBA.

Domos is going to introduce a new range of Health and Wellness soaps called "LUST FOR LIFE". This range will have a young active funky global image, and Domos wish to market the range in Europe as a first step. Domos' agency has set up a meeting in order to discuss a brand spokesperson pan-European endorsement contract.

The sports personality is a sports idol for young people in both the States and Europe who could sign contracts with a number of companies and has received other offers. However, s/he is interested in promoting his/her European image. His/her agent and manager both know s/he could get far more money in the States.

3. Role play the negotiation, following the agenda checklist. Useful phrases are provided.

_____ Relationship building: Get to know the other side, exchange personal and business information, establish an atmosphere of trust.

_____ Define the meeting and clarify the objectives.
- *To start with, we should establish the procedure.*
- *Is that acceptable to you?*
- *The purpose of this meeting is to ...*
- *By the end of this meeting we should have ...*

_____ State your opening position. Ask questions about the other side's position and interests. Listen. Do not start to bargain or negotiate at this stage; this is a phase of exploration.
- *Our main areas of concern are...*
- *Our priorities are ...*
- *In the short-term / mid-term / long- term we would like to ...*
- *What are your proposals?*
- *Why do you think that ...?*
- *Could you explain that in more detail?*

_____ Generate (creative) options and compromises considering both sides' positions. Hypothesising and brainstorming can be part of this phase.
- *If we did ..., what would you ...?*
- *Let's take a hypothetical situation ...*
- *What if ...?*
- *If we accepted that, would you be able to offer ...?*

_____ Bid and bargain. Put forward proposals considering all interests and parts of the final negotiated deal.
- *We are willing to ..., provided that you ...*
- *Are you willing to offer a compromise?*
- *How flexible are you on the question of ...?*
- *There is one condition though if we ...*
- *That's not viable but we would like to make an alternative proposal.*

_____ Agree. Summarise the agreement to clarify for both sides.
- *I think we are in agreement.*
- *We have a deal.*
- *Can we summarise what we have agreed?*

____ Close the meeting by signing the agreement, thanking and making closing remarks.
   - *It's been a pleasure doing business with you.*
   - *Here's to a happy and long-term relationship!*

WORD BANK: BRANDING

brand building: Improving the brand equity with advertising campaigns and/or promotions.

brand licensing: Leasing a brand name to another company; e.g., a computer company leasing its name to a company producing computer speakers.

brand portfolio: Total collection of trademarks used by a company with each brand usually having its own trademark; e.g., Domos has an unbeatable brand portfolio with a number of brands that are household names.

brand recall: How well consumers connect a type of product to a particular brand name, sometimes related to "household name"; e.g., consumers are asked in a survey to name as many cleaning products as possible, and 99% name CleanIT!

brand recognition: Consumers can identify the brand/product by just seeing a visual signal such as a logo, packaging, or advertising campaign.

brand sentiment: Consumers' (positive) feelings about the brand; e.g., Domos saw a significant rise in brand sentiment for Bright White after giving a free sample to every household.

brand stretching: Using an established brand name for unrelated products in a different category; e.g., using a well-known brand in the entertainment industry for insurance products.

brand switching: Consumer decision to break a bond of loyalty to a brand and buy a different brand.

2 CAMPAIGN MANAGEMENT

Introduction

The client employs the advertising agency, and they liaise to develop an advertising campaign. First, objectives and expectations are clarified. Then, a creative strategy is developed and a concept is developed and accepted. The concept is executed and placed on selected media. Finally, the results of the campaign are evaluated.

Watch five television commercials. Evaluate each one using the criteria below. Then describe two to a partner, one that you thought was effective and one that you thought was not.

1. What is the main idea or message?
2. Do you engage with the commercial? Why and when?
3. Do words, pictures, and/or music tell the story?
4. How is the story developed?
5. Does the commercial grab your attention? Why / Why not?
6. Is the commercial entertaining?
7. What does the commercial make you feel about the product / brand it is advertising?
8. What is the main selling idea?

A Vocabulary

1. Match the expressions (1-10) with their definitions (a- i).

1. tagline / strapline / slogan
2. business pitch
3. demographic descriptors
4. creative brief
5. values, attitudes, lifestyle, interests, VALS (values and lifestyle)
6. positioning statement
7. creative platform
8. copy (noun)
9. executional framework
10. voiceover

____ a. A sales presentation that is given in competition with other agencies or companies
____ b. Pyschographics
____ c. The story told in implementing the advertising strategy
____ d. A narration spoken in an advertisement without the speaker being seen; also called off-(screen) speaker
____ e. A description that incorporates the essence of what the brand stands for in relation to competitors' brands in the mind of the target audience
____ f. The written words in a print advertisement

____ g. A document giving an agency details on the brand, the company, and other relevant information
____ h. A short memorable phrase that sums up a brand's important characteristics
____ i. information about the target group; including, for example, age, income, and ratio of men to women
____ j. A document that provides creatives with a starting point by giving context, purpose, and focus

B Creative Brief / Briefing

1. Work with a partner. Explain why a creative brief is desirable.

2. The *New Campaign for CleanIT!* text represents an example of a creative brief. In this brief, underline and label:

a. client contact details
b. details on the media mix
c. market details
d. interesting background information
e. effect(s) the campaign should have
f. demographics
g. how consumers feel about the category

h. statements supporting the objectives
i. consumer insights
j. what must be done
k. brand personality
l. opportunities for the client to discuss creative input
m. the product's customer-oriented strengths

New Campaign for CleanIT!

Product Manager
Domos International
pm@domos.co.uk

Media Considerations
- TV: 30-second commercial clips – (national with roll-out to 10 European countries)
- Billboard Advertising
- Print
- Point of Sale (POS)

Overview
There have been 4 major players in the household cleaning sector with more or less equal market shares for approximately 25 years. The aim is to smash through this market configuration to establish CleanIT! as the No. 1 cleaning brand by value in the long-term by creating a relationship with children and teenagers that will lead to lifetime loyalty to CleanIT!, the brand of choice for 21st century consumers.

Campaign Objectives
The objective is to build on the success of the introduction of the Mr Super Clean character, who now becomes an instantly recognisable character associated with the CleanIT! brand and saving the planet. He communicates that CleanIT! can be purchased and used without any worries about harming the environment. Children, teenagers, and their parents should view Mr Super Clean as loveable, funky and cool - so much so that they will purchase future Mr Super Clean merchandising.

Target Market

The target group is everyone who uses cleaning products, and the core target group is males and females from the ages of 8 to 15 and their parents. Parents are both current and prospective users of CleanIT! and include mixed race, same sex and single parent households to reflect CleanIT!'s place in a multicultural, tolerant, 21st century society. Children, teenagers and parents probably have their concerns or feel guilty about purchasing and using certain cleaning products. It is likely that children even chastise their parents on their purchasing behaviour because they do not purchase cleaning products that are environmentally friendly.

Reasons to Believe

- CleanIT! was first developed in the 1900s and has a long heritage.
- Due to this long heritage, CleanIT! has a high level of expertise in cleaning.
- CleanIT! has always successfully adapted to changes in lifestyle and is known for innovation.
- CleanIT! has established itself as an environmentally friendly cleaning product of choice.
- In research, 90% children and consumers under the age of 25 gave "saving the planet" or "the environment" as their number 1 concerns for the future.
- Consumers reacted positively to the "Power to the Planet" campaign and to the Mr Super Clean character.

Consumer Benefit

You can use the cleaning power of CleanIT! with a 'clean' conscience but also ensure your home is sparkling clean.

What consumers told us

"I want to keep my home clean but don't want to use chemicals that harm my children or the environment. My children should be safe. In fact, they're always telling me when they think I'm destroying the planet. As parents, we have to look after the world we pass onto our children."

"I loved Mr Super Clean. He got across a serious and important message in a fun way. My young kids looked out for the advertisement on TV and searched for it on the Internet."

Mandatory

- Domos Logo
- Packshot

Further Information

Research and Development Environmental Report
R&D@domos.co.uk
Telephone 123 45678

Schedule

- Initial creative review of rough pencil sketch ideas / scribbles. (Date: _____)
- Review revised creative work. (Date: _____)
- Internal creative work presentation. (Date: _____)
- Final full creative & media presentation. (Date: _____)
- Final material delivered to broadcasters /publishers / website etc. (Date: _____)

packshot: A packshot is a moving or still image of the product being advertised showing the packaging, labelling and logo so that the viewer registers these.

C Creative Strategy

1. Read the definition of a message strategy. Then complete the descriptions of message strategies by circling the correct term.

> **Message strategy**: The message strategy defines the tactic or approach to deliver the theme of the advertising message. Message strategies can be summarised as being one of these types:
> - cognitive strategy (rational and logical)
> - conative strategy (direct response – call to action)
> - affective strategy (emotions and feelings)

a. (Comparative/Generic/Functional) claims must be true if you mention a competitor's name, to prevent lawsuits.

b. A (comparative/emotional/functional) strategy is one in which the Unique Selling Proposition (USP) is emphasised, giving a differentiated reason to buy one brand over another brand. This strategy can thus concentrate on features rather than benefits.

c. A (pre-emptive/generic/emotional) strategy is good for brand leaders because a brand is made synonymous with its product category.

d. A brand makes an assertion of superiority: "We are the best beer in the world", for example. Once the statement is made, it is difficult for the competition to make the same statement. This is a (pre-emptive/functional/comparative) strategy and is connected to hyperbole.

e. Romance, nostalgia, pleasure, fear, love, compassion, excitement, and joy are examples of a/an (functional/emotional/pre-emptive) strategy.

2. Read this definition of an ad appeal. Then match the ad appeal in the box with the correct features of the appeal (a-e).

> **Ad appeal:** The theme of the advertising message that forms the basis to connect and create relevance with the target audience. Each appeal is only suitable or effective for certain kinds of message.

> Rational, Fear, Humour, Scarcity, Music, Sex, Bandwagon, Emotion

_____ a. Head over heart
_____ b. Grabs attention, but fun side must be connected to the message
_____ c. Emphasises negative consequences of acting or not taking action; e.g., not taking insurance
_____ d. Jingles and songs linked to memories and experiences
_____ e. From romance to nudity; suggestiveness
_____ f. Appeals to the need to belong or the fear of missing out on something
_____ g. Heart over head
_____ h. Creates action by stressing there are limited supplies or a limited period of availability

3. Read this definition of an executional framework. Then match the label of a type of executional framework (1-9) with the correct description (a-i).

> **Executional framework**: The message strategy and ad appeal can then be matched to the manner in which the strategy is presented – the executional framework.

1. slice of life
2. authoritative
3. testimonial
4. dramatisation
5. fantasy
6. animation
7. personality symbol
8. demonstration
9. symbolic

_____a. Psychological differentiation building a world around the brand - important when product (e.g. petrol, tobacco) has little physical differentiation

_____b. Using expert(s) to talk about brand attributes and/or scientific evidence and/or expert knowledge

_____c. Identifying a central character with the product/brand by using an animation, spokesperson or animal

_____d. A story format

_____e. Showing how a product works by using it or staging the use of it

_____f. Not representing the real world – make- believe

_____g. Matches product to consumers' experiences – depicts a conflict or problem faced in daily life and the product solves the problem

_____h. Using characters drawn by an artist or by using computer graphics

_____i. A person speaks on behalf of a product talking about use and experience

4. Choose three current TVCs (television commercials) and identify the message strategy, ad appeal, and executional framework in each of them. Evaluate if the commercials are effective or not.

5. Suggest advertisements for the CleanIT! brand described in the creative brief in B on page 20 based on TVC 1-5:

TVC	message strategy	ad appeal	executional framework
	pre-emptive	humour	demonstration
	emotional	emotion	animation
	comparative	bandwagon	authoritative
	functional	fear	slice of life
	generic	rational	personality symbol

6. Would you suggest another creative strategy for the CleanIT! brand? Why?

7. Create a story for Mr Super Clean by:

- opening a page in an English dictionary and choosing the fifth word in the first column. Use this word as the basis for a story.
- choosing an object from a bag or box. Use this object as the basis for a story.
- choosing a picture from a random selection. Use this picture as the basis for a story.

D Execution

1. Complete the text *What's a Storyboard?* by writing the correct heading from the box.

application	elements	scheduling
background	presentation	shooting

What's a Storyboard?

1. _____

The storyboard technique originated in the film animation industry at Disney in the 1930s and has been adopted by the advertising industry. An advertising storyboard is a tool that is used to plan and present concepts for television commercials. A series of illustrations provides a representation of the finished commercial in its proposed sequence using a method similar to a comic book. It is a convenient method of showing a moving sequence without incurring the expense of filming.

2. _____

Creative teams in advertising agencies create commercials. A copywriter and art director work together to develop the ideas to meet the objectives outlined in the creative brief. When they have agreed on a strategy, they use a storyboard to work out their ideas in detail. A storyboard template provides a series of panels that the team uses to portray each scene or frame of the commercial with a sketch. The copywriter adds the appropriate words from the script to each frame.

3. _____

The storyboard depicts the different elements of the finished commercial, including video, still images, animation, sound effects and music.

4. _____

The creative team submits its storyboard for internal review and subsequent presentation to the client. A creative director in the agency reviews the storyboard and either approves it for presentation or suggests changes. The agency account executive presents the finished storyboard to the client, with the aim of gaining approval to proceed with production.

5. _____

Storyboards are also important for planning production of the commercial. The creative team works out the sequence and production requirements in detail. Television commercials can be produced in all kinds of length, but typically developed in slots such as 15, 30, and 60 seconds. The team calculates how many scenes it will need to tell the story within the available time together with the approximate length of each scene.

6. _____

The production version of the storyboard provides a visual brief for the director and/or production house who films the commercial. The storyboard is consulted to identify the necessary actors, props, and location. The director also checks the storyboard sequence to ensure there are no missing elements or scenes that would be difficult to shoot. Attention to detail at this stage helps prevent delays or incurring extra expenditure at the production stage.

Describing storyboards involves mastering vocabulary that describes countless situations and environments. It is advisable to check with a dictionary or thesaurus for every storyboard you need to describe and to rehearse presenting it.

2. Read this description of shooting locations:

> ## Shooting
> There are two possibilities:
> - Outdoor shoot – e.g. in the city, on the street, etc.
> - Indoor shoot – either the "studio shoot" (a clean hall where everything is built up with a set designer) or the "on location" shoot; e.g., offices, apartments, etc.

Then, brainstorm vocabulary to describe generic storyboards:

- landscapes
- buildings
- the weather

- the home
- the workplace
- dress

- being happy
- being sad
- being nervous
- being excited

Example:
"Krispy Cornflakes" 30 Secs.

1. *Open up on beautiful sunny morning in a modern family kitchen. The complete family is sitting around the breakfast table and the sun is streaming through the windows in the background. Everyone is laughing and enjoying a family breakfast together, evidently in a good mood.*
2. *Mum gets up and takes a carton of fresh cold milk from the refrigerator.*
3. *Reaction shot of Dad's face as he smiles.*

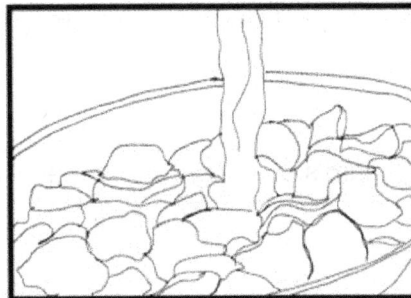

4. *Cut to daughter smiling as she watches Mum pouring the fresh milk over a bowl of the "Krispy Kornflakes".*
5. *Close up of milk pouring over the cornflakes which look refreshing and delicious.*
6. *The camera zooms out and we see the whole family enjoying their Krispy Kornflakes. VO: "Krispy Kornflakes – simply part of the family."*

2. Read the information about camera shots. Then match the name of the shot (1-10) with its correct description (a-i).

> **Camera shots**: These describe the amount of space that is seen in one shot or frame. They are used to demonstrate different aspects of setting, characters, and theme, thus shaping meaning.

1. Very wide shot
2. Wide shot
3. Close up

4. Reaction shot
5. Medium close up
6. Extreme close up

7. Mid-shot / Medium shot
8. Over the shoulder shot
9. Two-shot
10. POV

a. _____is also known as a noddy shot and shows a person's face listening or reacting to something.
b. _____is also known as an establishing shot. It shows the background, establishes the scene to put the rest of the film into context by showing the relationship between its important figures and objects. It is generally at the beginning of a scene to indicate where, and sometimes when, the remainder of the scene takes place.
c. _____means 'point of view', showing the action or scene from the eyes of one of the characters.
d. _____is used for conversation between equals, where what both characters say or do is equally important.
e. _____is used for conversation where one person's speech is more important than the other.
f. _____focuses on a single feature of a person such as the nose, mouth, hand or an object.
g. _____contains just one character's face focussing in on what one person has to say or shows reaction in facial expression.
h. _____concentrates attention on single character.
i. _____shows whole body putting the character in context to show location and how s/he relates to it.
j. _____is also known as the American shot and contains the characters or a character from the waist up.

3. Read the definition of camera angles. Then complete the descriptions (a-e) with the correct camera angle from the box.

> **Camera angles**: Used to position the viewer so as to understand the relationships between characters.

low angle	high angle	bird's eye angle	eye-level angle	Dutch angle

a. The angle from directly overhead establishing the scene or making people or objects appear small or insignificant is ____ ____ ____.
b. ____ ____ ____ puts the audience on an equal footing with the character/s.

    c. The angle that looks up at a character creating the feeling that the viewer is small and vulnerable and the character is powerful is _____ _____.

    d. The angle that looks down upon a subject creating the feeling that the character is smaller, less important, more vulnerable or being viewed by a more powerful presence is _____ _____.

    e. _____ _____ is when the camera is tilted to one side so the horizon is on an angle creating an interesting dramatic effect.

4. Match the camera setup used for different actions and emotions (1-6) with the correct description (a-f).

1. camera still on a tripod
2. steadicam
3. camera on a dolly

4. camera on a crane
5. handheld/ easy-rig
6. camera car

a. ____ A setup that is used for car chasing scenes.

b. ____ Using a locked camera needed for specific postproduction shots for example.

c. ____ A setup that is used to give the feeling of standing above the action.

d. ____ Using a mechanism for steadying a hand-held camera, consisting of a shock-absorbing arm to which the camera is attached and a harness worn by the camera operator, allowing a single operator to make smooth shots easily while still moving.

e. ____ Using a wheeled mount which enables the entire camera to move forwards or backwards - often used when recording a subject that moves away or toward the camera, in which case the goal is to keep the subject at the same distance from the camera.

f. ____ A setup that is used to give the feeling of being directly on the scene or to create the feeling of uneasiness.

5. Choose three current TVCs (television commercials) and analyse the camera shots, angles, and set ups.

E Creation

Create a TVC for CleanIT!, bearing the creative brief in **B** on page 20 in mind:

    a. Brainstorm ideas

    b. Evaluate those ideas

    c. Choose your best idea and create a narrative

    d. Prepare a script

    e. Work out in detail how the TVC moves from frame to frame

    f. Prepare a storyboard

F Pitch Presentation and Meeting

1. Read this description of an account executive.

> The **account executive** in the agency gets to know the business of the client so that s/he liaises and communicates ideas from the client to the agency's creative teams and vice versa. The role requires sales, negotiation, presentation, organising, and coordinating skills.

2. As agency account executive(s), pitch your TVC to the client, Domos. Tell the story and describe the camera angles and shots, locations, and settings, as well as the characters and emotions, to convince your client to proceed with production of the TVC. When you are not presenting, you represent the client Domos. Ask the agency some questions at the end of each presentation.

PITCHING TIP

Start on a high. Be enthusiastic and capture attention from the very beginning by making a jump start that is relevant to the presentation. You can use questions, a stunning quotation, surprising facts or statistics, tell the audience what they have to gain from listening to you (WIIFM – What's In It For Me?), or use another attention-grabbing technique. Maintain your passion and energy throughout and finish on a high. Finish with a bang using a technique that is again relevant to your pitch. Remember to summarise and give a clear take-home message, probably a call to action.

G TVC Production

1. Put these steps into the correct order for the procedure of TVC production.

a. _____ Shooting day(s).

b. _____ Fitting: Fitting of the models.

c. _____ Postproduction online: retouching and finalising the film, e.g. with the right logos, ending etc.

d. _____ Director's calls: talking to a chosen number (often at least three) of directors about the script and asking them to write their interpretation. Meanwhile the production house associated with this director will calculate the production costs.

e. _____ VO recording and mixing: recording the voice over (VO) and mixing it with the music and sound effects (sfx).

f. _____ PPM (Pre-Production Meeting): the agency, director, production house and client get together and the agency/ director present the options for cast, location, styling, props and decide on them.

g. _____ Briefing by creative and accounts.

h. _____ Station copies: sending out the final master films to the TV stations.

i. _____ Postproduction grading: giving the film a look by colour correcting each shot.

j. _____ Selection of the director whose interpretation fits best with the vision that the agency's creation and the client have, and cost approval by client in parallel.

k. _____ Pre-PPM (Pre-pre-production meeting): the agency, director and production house get together to discuss the director's ideas concerning the cast, location, styling, props, timing, etc.

l. _____ Recce (Reconnaissance): visiting all locations for the shooting (named Location Recce) and deciding on camera angles and positions (named Technical Recce).

m. _____Postproduction offline: editing the film and deciding on the edit.

n. _____ Research of directors that fit the product and idea of the film.

2. Check your answers by describing the process to a partner, like this: *First, the agency's …, Then, the agency, … After that, …* Switch roles with your roles after seven steps.

3.You are going to role play a PPM in three groups;- A (client), B (agency), and C (director/ production house). First, read the following description of a PPM.

PPM: A PPM (Pre-production meeting) is a meeting between the client, the agency, and the director /production house. This meeting is organised so that all parties are satisfied with the direction of an advertisement or campaign. It takes place a few days before the commercial is shot, so that there is enough time in case changes are required and they can be made and checked before the film is shot.

The contents of a PPM can be the agency treatments (script and storyboard), the director's shooting board, details about the cast, styling, location, the sets and props, moods, computer graphics references, production timing, and any post production steps such as music, sound effects, and voiceover.

4. Divide into three groups: A, B and C. In your group:

- meet to discuss the CleanIT! storyboard
- decide on the contents you wish to discuss and negotiate in the PPM.

All member of groups A, B, and C meet at the agency and negotiate the content and direction of the advertisement.

WORD BANK: CAMPAIGN MANAGEMENT

action safe: The area where it is safe to play the action so that it's visible on all different kind of TV screens.

AIDA: Attention, Interest, Desire, Action - historical model of how advertising works by getting attention, then interest, then desire and then action (purchase).

artwork: Visual elements of an advertisement.

billboard / hoarding: Outdoor sign or poster.

billings: Amount charged to clients including the agency commission, media and production costs, and so on.

camera pan: The camera is aimed sideways along a straight line. The camera itself does <u>not</u> move. It is often fixed on a tripod, with the operator turning it either left or right. Panning is commonly utilised to capture images of moving objects such as cars speeding or people walking.

camera tilt: Refers to the up or down movement of the camera while the camera itself does not move. Tilts are often employed to reveal vertical objects such as a building or a person.

channels of distribution: Routes used by a company to distribute products through wholesalers, retailers, mail order and so on.

clutter: The volume of advertising the consumer is exposed to forcing an advertisement to compete for attention.

consumer behaviour: Involves studying how people behave when selecting, using and disposing of products and services.

cut: A fast transition from one scene to another in film editing.

dissolve: A softer, more gradual transition from one scene to another in filming, often used to suggest a passage of time; e.g., from putting the washing in the washing machine to showing it hanging on the washing line, rather than showing the whole process in real time.

DOP: "Director of Photography" – the camera operator on a film set.

double/triple bid: Asking 2 or 3 directors/production houses to interpret and calculate the script.

eye tracking: A research method that determines what part of an advertisement is looked at by tracking the pattern of eye movements.

frames per second: One real time second consists of 25 frames.

frequency: The number of times an average person or home is exposed to media in a given time period.

jump cut: A technique which allows the editor to jump forward in time.

key visual: A visual image that encapsulates the tonality of a brand or product, what it stands for, and what people should think or feel about that product or brand.

infomercial: A TV commercial that is similar in presentation to a news programme or talk show, promoting a product in a style that appears objective.

layout: A drawing showing the relative positions of headline, photo, logo, body copy, etc. in an advertisement.

mood film: An arrangement of scenes depicting the look and feel of the film but does not necessarily portray the exact story.

mood board: An arrangement of key images, texts, and material on one visual to stimulate and convey the style and concept of an advertisement

OTS: "Opportunity To See" – quantifying how many exposures/the average frequency should be planned for a campaign.

post testing: Testing the effects of an advertisement *after* it has appeared in media.

reach: The percentage of a target audience exposed at least once to an advertising message during a given time period.

rough cut: A first version of film that is cut and edited without voiceover or music.

title safe: The area where it is safe to place titles so they do not get cut off on a TV screen.

watercooler effect: Occurs when a large number of people gather and talk about a TV programme.

3 BELOW THE LINE

Introduction

The expressions **above the line** and **below the line** originated at the Procter & Gamble company in 1954 and were originally developed to distinguish two methods of payment to advertising agencies, fixed fees, or payment for promotional activities. Above the line and below the line are now generally applied to differentiate these two kinds of promotional campaign.

> **Above the line (ATL)**: Uses mass media to promote brands and build brand awareness. *Example*: CleanIT! TV campaign.
>
> **Below the line (BTL)**: Uses other media to promote products directly to consumers and drive individual response. *Example*: Vouchers handed out to commuters that can be used to get a free bottle of CleanIT! at a local store.
>
> **Through the line (TTL)**: Uses both above and below the line communications, so that one form of advertising points the consumer to another form of advertising, thus "crossing the line". This refers to an advertising strategy that adopts a more integrated approach. *Example*: TV advertising for CleanIT! promoting consumers to sample the product at a retail outlet where they are given a competition entry form.

Discuss these statements:

- "ATL and BTL are antiquated, outdated terms if we consider the Internet and the speed of change in communication."
- "True innovation and creativity are only found in BTL activities today."
- "Digital communication has broken the division between ATL and BTL."
- "It is frustrating, confusing, and time wasting when a client still insists on making a distinction between ATL and BTL."
- "I would only recommend BTL activities to a client with a niche market."
- "Today people watch TV but engage online about the content at the same time. The line between ATL and BTL has become completely blurred."

A Vocabulary

1. Write the words and expressions in the most appropriate category. Then discuss your choices with a partner or group. Did you always agree?

sampling, print, broad reach, events, impulse purchasing, insights into ROI (return on investment), image, measurable, quantifiable, POS (point of sale), blurring of the line, radio, direct mail, integrated communication, targeted, cost-effective, category leader, followers, macro, personal, consistency (of content), PR (public relations), branding, specific, multiple points, outdoor, engagement, likes, awareness, TV, challenger brand, conventional, micro, gross ratings, trackable

Above the Line	Below the Line	Below the Line

B Direct Mail

1. Read the text *Personalisation is a Must*. Then answer the questions with a partner.

a. What is a triggered email?
b. What is an abandoned cart email?
c. What are the criteria for creating good direct email?

Personalisation is a Must

Direct Mail Publications interviewed Katie Harrison, Director at Baby Connect, a Domos E-commerce company that sells baby gifts tied in with Domos product ranges for babies.

DMP: What's different about shopping at Baby Connect?
KH: People shop with us because they have a specific need. A friend or a relative has a baby and people want to send something very personal rather than some generic gift. Personalisation is part of our DNA.
DMP: And what does that mean for you as a marketer?
KH: Simply that our marketing messages have to complement this need for personalisation, and we must have the resources to do this.
DMP: What kind of messages in detail?
KH: 'Triggered email' is email that is sent in response to a specific behaviour on the website, such as a thank you message or a shipping confirmation. It's all about sending the right content at the right time - being relevant and timely. An 'abandoned cart email' is sent to a lost customer, one who quit the online shopping cart before completing the sale, so that we can recover the sale.
DMP: What helps you to create personalised messages?
KH: We use the best tools and invest in software that is state-of-the-art. This enables us to identify purchase histories, browsing patterns and IP addresses so that we can create more personalised messages. Timing is essential, and we have to ensure that a shopper has an interest or intent at the moment we are communicating with him or her. Content also plays a significant role. We need to show products that the shopper has expressed an interest in but also to make suggestions to match the shopper's interests.

DMP: Do you have a final message for our readers?
KH: Marketers need to address customers in a personalised way. This can depend on the product and service of course, but it is increasingly expected that messages are tailored to the individual customer. My opinion is that personalisation is no longer a choice but a must.

2. Find three examples of triggered email (welcome; confirmation; unsubscribe; date-based - e.g. birthday or anniversary; thank you; complete action - e.g. install software; inactivity). Analyse the emails. Identify elements that make the emails effective or ineffective.

3. Write a shipping confirmation email on behalf of Baby Connect to a customer who bought a personalised baby girl bedtime gift box.

C Public Relations

1. Read the text *Writing a Press Release*, and write one of headings in the appropriate place for each paragraph.

Avoid Specialist Language	Make Sure It's Newsworthy	Style
Check It	Shorter Is Sweeter	The Beginning
Include Quotations	So, What Are Press Releases?	The Last Paragraph
'Inverted Pyramid'		

Writing a Press Release

1. _____

Press releases are a written presentation of facts that brands, businesses and organisations use to reach their target audience through the media by announcing stories about product launches, awards, events, achievements and so on. Releases are written internally or externally by a PR specialist or agency and sent to journalists and editors to publish. Here are some tips on writing press releases.

2. _____

Firstly, it is important to attract attention and ensure there is actually a story to tell. A human interest, unconventional, or provocative story demands attention and will be read.

3. _____

The headline acts as a teaser to the content of the release and should catch the eye. It needs to give an overview or summary of the story and encourage people to read the rest of the release.

4. _____

Then, the release should be written in the third person unless using direct quotes from other people. Statements such as "We did this" or "I think that" should be avoided. Copy written specifically for a website or company newsletter does not work for a press release as it is likely to be written in the first person, without journalists or the final reader in mind, and to be too self-promotional.

5. _____

Stories can be cut short by editors or journalists. Therefore, introduce the essential information at the beginning and use the following paragraphs to elaborate and provide evidence. Structuring the press release in order of declining importance ensures the most important information is included at the beginning and will not be missed by editors or journalists.

6. _____

Journalists want key points, facts and figures. If the release leaves them wanting to know more, they might make contact to ask for more details. Key information can be included by answering the five W questions: Who has done something? What have they done? Where did they do it? When did they do it? Why is it important?

7. _____

Terminology should be kept simple and easy to understand. A good idea is not to use jargon and to explain news as if talking to a friend. If the use of technical terms or abbreviations is unavoidable, the meaning of these terms should be explained.

8. _____

Soundbites are short quotations that encapsulate a message in very few words and capture the essence of a story. They provide credibility and evidence and often act as interview content if journalists lack the resources to follow up the release with an additional interview. Quotations should be kept positive, upbeat and to the point.

9. _____

It cannot be assumed that journalists know a company, organisation, or a person. An "about" section should be included, giving details of the company or organisation so that journalists are not given the extra work of researching this information. This section usually comes at the end of the press release and can be called a boilerplate.

10. _____

Proofreading is essential, especially if the press release is written in English and this is not the writer's first language. This includes looking for spelling, grammar, and punctuation mistakes. It is also important to review the accuracy of the content because once a press release has been released, it is in the public domain, and an editor or journalist may print it as a finished article.

2. Read the description of the corporate communications department. Then do the exercise that follows.

Corporate Communications: The department integrated in a company that is responsible for public relations as part of the company's strategic objectives.

a. You work for the Corporate Communications Department at Domos. Your boss has left this note on your desk:

Press release in English today

"Power to the Planet" campaign
Mr Super Clean — what a charming
character — Families will love him.
Merchandising to follow next year.

CleanIT! — BEST cleaner ever!!
Blah Blah on Domos.

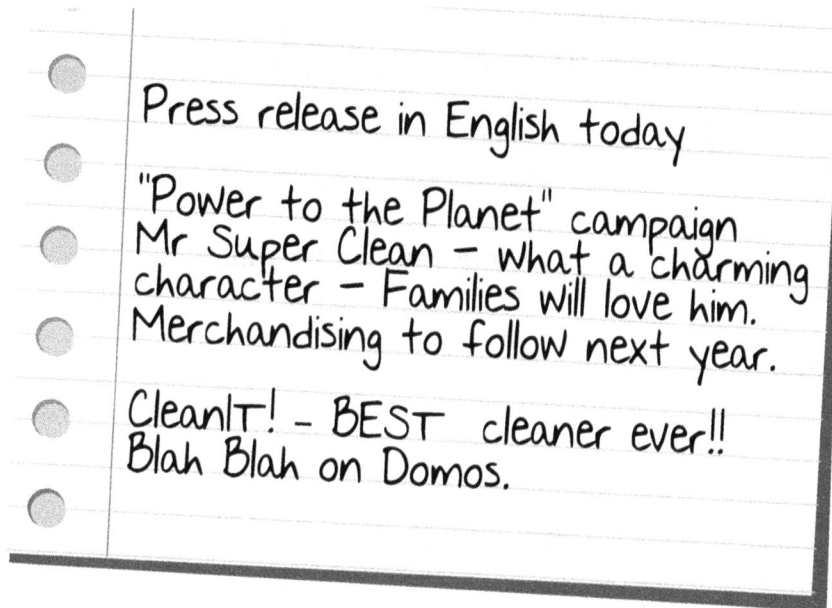

b. You assign the task to an intern, who writes the following press release. Evaluate it and give feedback to the intern in light of the text *Writing a Press Release*.

Domos Announces Mr Super Clean

Do the planet a favour and buy CleanIT! in a 1 litre or 2 litre bottle from your nearest supermarket. Domos is a big manufacturer of washing poweders since many years and now announces CleanIT! with Mr Super Clean. He is charming. The global headquarter are in the United Kingdom.

The CEO said, "We are proud for our new offer. CleanIT! is a new innovative product but with a long heritage". CleanIT! is the best cleaner ever.

Paula McInfrey is a spokesperson. She says, "The product is for people just like me. Intelligent and caring but you do not want to clean".

The TV campagne will start on all channels tonight. The name is "Power to the Planet" and we think it is very good. The family will all be loving him. So, go to the supermarket and buy the merchandising and get your freebies.

c. Write a new, improved press release for your boss.

D Event Marketing

1. Read the information about event marketing.

Event marketing involves designing and creating a marketing activity or occasion to promote a product or brand. This includes running marketing events at sports games, music festivals, or concerts, but also organising events such as sampling at a local store or corporate hospitality.

2. Discuss these questions with a group.

    a. Have you ever worked in event marketing? If so, how would you describe your experience?

    b. Describe event marketing that you have experienced as a consumer.

    c. What other types of event can you suggest?

    d. What aspects need to be considered before deciding on an event?

    e. What are the aims of event marketing?

    f. What aspects should an event manager consider during the running of an event?

    g. What aspects should be considered after an event?

3. You are going to role play a meeting. Work in small groups. Each group should read one of the events (1-4) below. Prepare a full description of your event, and develop arguments that support its implementation.

CleanIT Briefing

The core target market is males and females from the ages of 8 to 15 and their parents. Parents are both current and prospective users of CleanIT! and include mixed race, same sex, or single parent households to reflect CleanIT!'s place in a multicultural, tolerant, 21st century society. Children, teenagers, and parents probably have concerns or feel guilty about purchasing and using certain cleaning products. It is likely that children even chastise their parents on their purchasing behaviour.

Mr Super Clean is cool. He cares. If you care about the planet, then you should do what Mr Super Clean does and make CleanIT! the household cleaning brand of choice. Mr Super Clean is fun and dynamic. CleanIT! has always been innovative. Your grandparents trusted CleanIT! and you can trust the brand too. CleanIT! has a long heritage but adapts to the modern world. CleanIT! is therefore traditional and modern at the same time.

a. You work at the agency that handles Domos as a client. As part of the BTL budget, you are planning an event. So far, these proposals have been put forward:

Event 1: Primary Schools
Target of 100 schools. A fun event with competitions and games for children aged 8 - 11 with a "caring for the environment" theme. All children receive freebies – a Mr Super Clean stuffed toy and a T-shirt.

Event 2: City Centre Supermarkets
A light-hearted demonstration of the power of CleanIT! with models dressed as Mr Super Clean cleaning everything they possibly can - supermarket shelves, shopping trollies, baby buggies, etc. The dirtiest car brought to the supermarket and then cleaned by using CleanIT! wins a year's supply of free Clean IT!

Event 3: City Centre Train Stations
Models dressed as well-known superheroes take over the train stations at busy commuting periods. They act as superheroes helping people from trains, giving out free coffee, climbing over the station facilities, etc. Mr Super Clean enters, "cleans" the other superheroes away, and gives out free samples of CleanIT!

> **Event 4: The 10th annual 'J' Music Festival**
> CleanIT! staff clean public areas and are very visible throughout the festival. They run a "clean your tent" activity and give out free samples of CleanIT! In addition, a large public tent offers festival goers a CleanIT! chill out zone where they can relax in a calm, clean, harmonious environment with sounds of the ocean, whales, and other natural sounds.

b. Meet as the agency to plan the event. This is the agenda:

Agenda

1. Proposals for events
2. Advantages and disadvantages of each proposal
3. Selection of event
4. Next steps
5. A.O.B. (any other business)

---

c. Write a press release reporting the event.

E Pitch Presentation

1. Read this job advertisement.

Job Vacancy – Direct Marketing Manager
International Overseas Aid Charity

This is a fantastic opportunity to use your marketing education and skills to promote humanitarian aid and work in an environment that provides true job satisfaction. Responsibilities include developing and managing both digital and offline direct marketing strategies and implementing these strategies during fund raising drives for major disasters or emergencies.

Our direct marketing is primarily aimed at current supporters and must be timely and relevant. You will be required to manage external agencies, implement innovative digital and offline programmes, maintain good press relations, supervise both outdoor and direct mail activities, design activities to increase supporter numbers, and be responsible for budget and financial planning.

We are looking for someone who has been educated in marketing communications to degree level. Experience with marketing techniques in press strategy, media relations, direct mail, telemarketing and digital marketing is desirable. Applicants should be able to demonstrate excellent project management skills and the ability to remain calm and decisive under pressure.

2. You have applied for the job outlined in the advertisement and receive this email:

Dear Candidate,

Thank you for your recent application for the post of Direct Marketing Manager. We are delighted to inform you that you have been put on the shortlist of candidates for interview.

As part of the selection process, please prepare a 10-minute pitch outlining your ideas for an innovative direct marketing campaign aimed at our charity's current supporters after an earthquake. You will give this pitch to a panel at the start of your interview.

Further details and directions to our headquarters are given in the attachment. We would be grateful if you could confirm your attendance at the interview.

Regards,
Human Resources
International Overseas Aid Charity.

Prepare and give the 10-minute pitch.

PITCHING TIPS

Don't spend the hours immediately before your pitch changing ideas, structure, and visual aid materials or adding more and more detail. If you are confused, then your client will be too.

Design your pitch and then rehearse, rehearse, rehearse. Familiarise yourself with your material and get your timing right. Check the logical flow of your argumentation because logical flow reduces the amount of working memory needed to follow your presentation. If your client follows your flow, you will have a much greater chance of selling yourself and your ideas.

Then, rehearse with a colleague or a friend. Get a second opinion on what works, what doesn't work, and what should be added or removed, so that you can make any necessary adjustments.

Have a final rehearsal about 24 hours before your pitch so that you start the pitch to the client feeling refreshed and confident. By this stage, you'll know your material thoroughly. Practice really does make perfect.

WORD BANK: BELOW THE LINE

challenger brand: A brand that is not the category leader and fights against the position of the category leader.

clippings: Copies of media content for the client.

community relations: Building and enhancing relations and fostering understanding of the role of a company in the local community.

conversion rate: The percentage of responders to a direct mailing action who become customers.

editorial calendar: A listing of planned future themes and features in a publication.

embargo: An agreement that a press release or other publication will not be published until a specific time or date; e.g., announcing a new invention "under embargo" so that all publications have equal access and clients receive the news from multiple sources at the same time.

envelope stuffer: Including a direct mail message with another message such as a bill sent by mail.

hit: The achievement of media coverage.

in-house magazine / newsletter: Tool to communicate with employees about news, issues and developments.

list maintenance: Keeping a mailing list current by correcting and updating addresses and other data.

lobbying: Public relations communication involving relations with government or official organisations using political intelligence and pressure.

mailing list: List of customers or prospects (potential customers) to send catalogues or announcements to.

niche marketing: Finding a product that appeals to only one group and selling that product profitably only to that group.

prospecting: Mailing or telemarketing potential customers to buy for the first time.

media list: List of the media relevant to a company, news story, or campaign; - i.e., the journalists who might want to run a story.

media monitoring: Observing and checking coverage in the press and on TV, radio, and the Internet.

media relations: Dealing with and building up good working relationships with journalists.

print production: The process of producing printed material such as brochures, posters, and leaflets.

publics: Groups of people who face a problem or have an issue with a company or organisation. A PR term, publics are identified and classified according to the extent the groups are aware of the problem and the action they take.

reactivation: A programme encouraging lapsed customers to start buying again.

respondent: A person who has answered a direct response letter or advertisement.

response rate: The percentage of people who responded to an offer.

relationship marketing: Building connections with customers which results in customers becoming more loyal and purchasing more.

stakeholders: People or groups who have an interest in company or organisation - employees, creditors, suppliers, community, shareholders, etc.

traction: The act of getting widespread media coverage.

4 PROMOTION

Introduction

Sales promotions are temporary activities and incentives that make a product or service more attractive to new customers, stimulating and increasing demand and / or improving product availability in the short-term. Sales promotions include coupons, discounts, contests, point of sale displays, trade fairs etc.. Customers are final consumers, the retail or wholesale trade. Sales promotion is a promotional tool that belongs to Promotion, one of the four Ps of the marketing mix, that integrates well with the other three Ps: Product, Price, and Place.

Discuss these statements:

- "Not all discounts are in the buyer's favour."
- "Consumers look for promotions before making a purchasing decision destroying brand loyalty."
- "Sales promotions are more important than advertising as the purchasing decision is really made at the point of sale."
- "Sales promotions shift focus from the product itself and damage product differentiation."
- "Sales promotions are lazy because they lack imagination, creativity, and innovation."
- "Sales promotions are short-term and damage a brand in the long-term."

A Vocabulary: Sales Promotion

1. Match the objective (1-8) with the sales promotion (a-h).

1. to stimulate trial of the product
2. to lock customers into a loyalty programme
3. to reward loyal customers
4. to target a specific group
5. to generate publicity
6. to encourage a repeat purchase
7. to build a customer database
8. to bring the realisation of change or repositioning to the consumer

a. ____ Here's a cheque for 200 Euros to spend at your GMW dealer. No catch. Simply a gift from GMW cars to say thank you for choosing to buy another GMW.

b. ____ If you're ready to embrace a whole new look, why not download our voucher and try out the new Reon eyeliner at no cost to you whatsoever?

c. ____ Every household will receive a free sample of our new mild concentrated formula Xtreme washing liquid to see just how effective it is.

d. ____ Enter our free draw for a two-week holiday in the Bahamas by filling in your personal details on the online form and submitting it.

e. ____ Use this coupon to get 50% off when you next buy this product.

f. ____ With our Club Points Plus card, you can accelerate your rewards and quickly achieve Elite Status. Redeem 250 points for a free night at any of hotels worldwide.

g. ____ To all football fans - enjoy the match and get a cup of steaming hot Choco at half time. Buy 4 cups and claim your free team T-shirt.

h. ____ Come to Maxi Electronics on Saturday and join in our karaoke competition with the well known rapper I.M. Vile appearing as a judge. The winner gets a new 60" state-of-the-art TV. Get online and tell your friends to come along too!

B Marketing Roles

1. Match the person or institution in (1-6) to the comments in (a-f):

1. Institute of Marketing
2. A manager at a major telecommunications company
3. Advertising Standards Authority
4. Marketing Manager at a shopping mall
5. A consumer
6. President of Marketing at a record label

a. ____ "All kinds of companies pester me with unwanted marketing messages on my smartphone. Sometimes I just feel bombarded with information. It really annoys me and actually puts me off the companies that do this. All in all, it is nothing but a new form of cold calling."

b. ____ "We offer free wifi to increase footfall. Over 55% of those who sign up for wifi opt in to receive direct marketing messages. Then, we collate information and ensure that we only send out relevant messages so that we create affinity. For example, we contact parents of young children if a kids' TV personality is appearing at the mall. Shoppers also use wifi to share their own content, such as posting photos of the mall or news or stories about what they've bought. This is extremely effective, but we do not rely only on digital but also use integrated marketing communications campaigns with advertisements on digital screens around the mall, print advertising in the local press, flyers, giveaways, free samples and competitions."

c. ____ "Our objective is to be the number one mobile network provider. Research shows that mobile phones and tablets have become the new personal shopper for many consumers who compare prices online or get a second opinion via social media. We have therefore introduced a digital loyalty reward programme to attract prospects. This takes the form of a range of consumer sales promotions including discounts, BOGOFs (Buy One Get One Free), freebies, and coupons that are exclusive to our customers and can be used in both major High Street and online stores."

d. ____ "The digital strategy is to concentrate on the long-term, to warm consumers to our brand, and to create fans. We are not in the business of using gimmicks that simply have a short-term or even negative effect. We aim to encourage consumers to try out content. The challenge is to have the right content in the right place at the right time. We are just as happy with someone viewing a video online as we are with selling to that person. Engagement is key and will naturally lead to upselling at some point in the future."

e. ____ "Our recommendation to marketers is that they should keep pace with consumer adoption of new technologies. If brands send too many messages, they perpetuate the associations of spam and junk. This will lead to consumers ultimately rejecting marketing techniques."

f. ____ "Brands are obliged to tell people what data they are collecting and what might be done with it. They must also give consumers the opportunity to opt out, and ensure that messages are sent in the right context in short and understandable formats. Brands should also consider what constitutes a breach of privacy."

2. In comment a above, circle the words or expressions that mean:

    a. to bother with demands

    b. contact by telephone when the receiver has not given permission to do this

In comment b, circle the words or expressions that mean:

    a. to choose something

    b. meaningful connection between a group of people and the offer made to them

    c. product that does not cost anything

    d. measurement of number of people entering a shop or mall in a period of time

    e. campaign that is part advertisement and part sales promotion

In comment c, circle the words or expressions that mean:

    a. two products for the price of one

    b. potential customer

In comment d, circle the words or expressions that mean:

    a. trick to attract attention in an attempt to sell

    b. purchasing more expensive items, upgrades or add-ons

In comment e, circle the words or expressions that mean:

    a. unwanted; of little use or value

    b. to make something continue to exist for a long time

In comment f, circle the words or expressions that mean:

    a. to choose not to take part

    b. infringement

C Promotions Through the Years

1. Read the following case studies that describe both unsuccessful and successful promotional campaigns. Then, answer the question at the end of each case study.

1995

Two young ambitious marketing executives at WashPool, a British market leader for white goods, had an incredible idea and believed this would ensure their careers for the rest of their lives. Their idea actually finished their careers together with that of their CEO, Ivor Cropper, and almost destroyed the company they worked for. WashPool was eventually taken over by the Swedish giant, HF Appliances, and subsequently became a minor brand. What happened?

The idea was simple. British consumers were offered a free two-week holiday in Spain or France if they bought a WashPool product for at least £100. However, one of the first rule of promotions is never to offer anything that is seen to be worth more than the product it is promoting. It did not take long for consumers to work out that a holiday was worth more than a cheap appliance. Sales of the WashPool 5000 tumble dryer, priced at £119 and the cheapest appliance to qualify for the promotion, rocketed. WashPool failed to put any kind of limit or cap on the promotion and consumers continued to demand free holidays well into 1996.

Thousands of British households bought appliances they didn't really need. Newspapers were full of small ads for appliances that nobody could use. In fact, WashPool succeeded in flooding the market for its own products. The company generated short-term sales of £35 million but had to spend over £55 million on the free holidays. WashPool was the market leader and could have withstood this painful financial loss over time, but it was actually the public image disaster that eventually killed the company.

How did the company make such a huge mistake?

1988

As a global brand, Giant Burger has been an official sponsor of the World Adventure Games since 1972 and consistently one of the world's top advertisers. During the Games in 1980, Giant Burger ran a promotion in its domestic market in the United States by giving away a gigantic burger to every customer for every gold medal that the US won. A silver medal resulted in a free portion of fried potatoes and a bronze meant a soft drink. This promotion was a success since the company was able to cross-sell to the majority of people who claimed free food, and Giant Burger generated a lot of positive PR. The company decided to run the same promotion for the 1988 World Adventure Games.

However, this time Americans won many more medals than Giant Burger had predicted. The demand for the promotion was so immense that Giant Burger restaurants in the States did not have enough food to cover the demand. Giant Burger's PR machine came into operation. It was widely suspected that Giant Burger sustained a loss on the two-week promotion, but the company was able to keep a lid on the precise numbers. PR spin doctors managed to turn a potentially negative story into a positive one by celebrating America's achievements and linking them to the company's success. The expenditure must have been heavy at the time, but Giant Burger is still a major sponsor of the World Adventure Games today, and its name is very much connected with this global event in the minds of the consumer.

What did Giant Burger get right and wrong?

2010

In response to slumping sales and bad publicity about fried foods, Big Fry Fast Foods (BFFF) decided to put a new low calorie "Slim" range on its menu in 2010. In order to promote its new range in the United States, BFFF decided to offer a free sample of its new menu to those who produced a coupon that could be downloaded from the Internet. The promotion ran for the whole of the month of May.

At the same time, BFFF contracted Paula McInfrey, one of America's major TV stars, to be a spokesperson for the new range of products. BFFF did not disclose the full details of the contract with Paula McInfrey, but she must have received a substantial fee. On her TV show on May 2, Paula gave details of the new "Slim" products. She then mentioned briefly that consumers could have a free sample of the menu, giving details of the website where the coupon could be found.

The primary audience for the announcement was already large but the secondary audience was huge. Those who had seen the TV programme quickly contacted friends and family using social media so that the news of the promotion spread like wildfire. BFFF restaurants were simply overwhelmed by the number of coupons presented to them, and they ran out of food in three days.

Negative publicity quickly followed with TV reports, and Internet bloggers reported extremely angry consumers in long queues at BFFF restaurants. Newspaper reports then began to question the credibility of BFFF introducing a "Slim" range when the restaurant chain was known for its fried fast food.

After five days, the website with the downloadable coupon crashed.

BFFF tried to spin the story by claiming that the new range was so popular and in such high demand that stocks had run dry. This was not effective. BFFF was offering a giveaway and could not supply it. Consumers were not persuaded by BFFF's counter measures and the company was unable to counteract the negative publicity.

By May 15, the website was up and running again, and stocks of the new range were fully replenished at BFFF restaurants. The damage had already been done, and BFFF's efforts to recover the situation were not widely or sympathetically reported. The "Slim" range was removed from BFFF's menu at the beginning of 2013.

Could the promotion for "Slim" have been handled more effectively?

2015

Highton in London's suburbs is the home of the world famous children's author, Jennifer Bristow. The writer spent many hours in the local café drafting her first book, *The Mastery of Freddie Flixton*. She has often stated in interviews that she will be eternally grateful to the coffee shop and will never forget the staff's friendliness and patience. With Jennifer's permission and full blessing, the coffee shop renamed itself 'Freddie's Place' in 2012.

Martha Freeman, the café's owner, does not have a marketing background. She just sells great coffee, served with a smile in a wonderful homely atmosphere. One day in 2013, Martha was playing around with the new logo for Freddie's Place and testing to see if it worked in black and white on photocopies. She then had a brilliant promotional idea.

The offer was simply this: Applicants had to sign a contract stating that they would dress and live as the Freddie character depicted on the logo for a month. In return, each applicant would receive free coffee at the café for ten years. Martha thought it unlikely that many people would take up the offer – who would want to dress like Freddie for a month? – but nevertheless capped the offer at the first fifty applicants.

Martha was inundated with applications, and the publicity generated by the stunt was immense. Videos of Freddie characters at work in offices and factories, drinking in pubs and going shopping went viral. The story was picked up by national press and TV and then by international media, so that Martha and her 'Freddies' became media stars.

Some experts said the stunt would eventually backfire because the café would lose money if fifty applicants took free coffee every day. There are indeed a handful of the fifty 'Freddies' who come to the café on a daily basis, but they take great pleasure in sometimes dressing as Freddie for tourists, generating further publicity for the café. Some 'Freddies' have moved from the Highton area, and some just take a coffee every few weeks or so. The promotion has more than paid for itself. 'Freddie's Place' now successfully sells Freddie merchandise and has expanded to five outlets around London since the promotion was created.

Why was Martha Freeman so successful?

D Pitch Presentation

1. Work in pairs or small groups. As an agency, create a sales promotion for CleanIT!. Pitch your ideas to your client, Domos.

While you are watching sales promotion pitches from other pairs or groups, represent the client Domos. Ask the agency questions.

PITCHING TIP

Cognitive Load Theory tells us that working memory is limited, so we can only take in a limited amount of information when it is presented. Sharpen your pitch by cutting down on complexity, keeping things simple, breaking down information, using visual materials effectively, and providing context.

E Packaging: The Silent Salesman

1. Name some brands you recall because of these features of the packaging:

- shape
- image
- distinctiveness
- colour
- typeface

- size
- materials
- a graphic element
- simplicity
- functionality

2. Describe brand packaging you recall that:

- is environmentally friendly
- has a retro look and/or feel
- disrupts the category
- is quirky
- is global

3. Complete the text on colour using words from this box:

> amendments, appropriate, attached to, differentiate, distinguish, effectiveness, enhance, essential, inappropriate, mirror, purpose, strategic, subjective, subliminal messages, target market.

Colour

Colour impacts our thoughts and behaviour and is thus an (1) _____component of packaging design, adding a visual element which can (2) _____image and branding. Therefore, companies and organisations should try to select colours that (3) _____brands and products and (4) _____them.

When choosing colours, marketers need to determine the (5) _____of the product or brand and keep the (6) _____in mind. Colour should relate to the message behind a logo and

(7) _____any intended image. It can be a mistake just to choose a favourite colour without checking the (8) _____behind the colour. A marketer might decide on a colour but discover that it is actually (9) _____for the brand. However, rules can be broken, and we can all recall examples of brands not following conventions for (10) _____reasons.

Some colours are just simply unsuitable, though. It is highly unlikely that a marketer would select blue packaging for a food product containing banana or green for a cherry drink. Yellow and red are clearly the (11) _____colours. The impact of colour is (12) _____, and not all people react to colours in the same way. Personalities differ, as do the ways we use language and our senses. Accordingly, it is definitely advisable to research any cultural preferences and cultural meanings (13) _____colours, again keeping the target consumers in mind.

Finally, companies and organisations should test the (14) _____of chosen colours and be prepared to make any necessary (15) _____.

4. Which subliminal messages or associations would you associate with these colours?

| a. white | c. blue | e. green | g. yellow | i. magenta |
| b. black | d. red | f. orange | h. purple | j. pink |

These words may help:

nouns		adjectives	
abundance	optimism	affordable	indecisive
anger	passion	authoritative	inspiring
balance	prohibition	brash	masculine
confidence	prosperity	classy	non-threatening
courage	protection	comforting	outrageous
extravagance	purity	dependable	over-the-top
growth	royalty	elegant	reliable
honesty	security	enthusiastic	religious
ignorance	serenity	extroverted	shocking
innocence	sophistication	glamorous	superior
integrity	spirituality	gloomy	unadventurous
longevity	strength	harmonious	uninhibited
loyalty	tranquillity	healthy	uplifting
luxury	warning	imaginative	vital
mystery	wisdom	immature	weak

5. Categorise the following as physical or psychological functions of packaging:

authenticity, convenience, distinctiveness, emotion, grabbing attention, handling, information, instruction, manifestation of brand, motivation, protection, reflecting brand personality, signifying value, symbolism, trust

physical functions	psychological functions

6. Collect four or five examples of packaging. Present each to the whole group explaining elements that make the packaging effective or ineffective.

F Trade Fairs

1. Read the text about an annual trade fair.

DISCOVERY NY FAIR

Discovery NY is the world's largest annual trade fair for FMCG (Fast Moving Consumer Goods), and all eyes will be on New York again this year. Discovery provides FMCG manufacturers with a unique platform to test and launch new products, increase brand awareness, and build international business contacts in the retail and wholesale sectors. Over 77% of visitors come from international markets outside the USA. Don't miss out! Book your stand today at www.discoveryNY.com/participation.

Domos exhibit at Discovery NY every year. The target this year is to increase traffic to the Domos stand by 30% on last year. The stand and exhibits should attract attention and create a wow factor, generating as much publicity as possible. "Wow" factor ideas could include an innovative product demonstration, a meet a celebrity event, giveaways, a VIP area, a competition, or...?

Read the description of a press/media kit:

Press Kit / Media Kit: A packaged set of promotional and news materials which is distributed to the media. For example, a kit could include a historical and statistical fact sheet about the company, a biography of the CEO, photos of the management board, a current press release, a DVD promoting new innovations, and media contact information for the Corporate Communications Department.

2. You work for the Corporate Communications Department at Domos. Write each of these:

1. A private invitation to the editor of the magazine FMCG Today, offering a personal visit to the Domos stand and enclosing a press/media kit.
2. An email invitation to existing clients, offering a 10% discount on purchases made at the trade fair.

3. An announcement of the Domos stand for social media with the aim of creating buzz (energy, excitement, or anticipation).
4. A press release announcing Domos' stand and exhibits this year.

G Report Writing

1. Read the text below to find out about mystery shoppers.

What Is She Doing?

If you see Janet Browhall next to you in the queue at the supermarket checkout counter and look very closely, you'll notice that she's not checking items off a shopping list but is making notes about the appearance of the store, the length of time waiting in the checkout line, and the point of sale displays. Why?

Janet is a mystery shopper for Shopper Market Experts, a specialist agency which works for a number of major retailers who seek to measure the experience that shoppers have in brick and mortar stores. Shopper Market Experts assign different store locations to each of their mystery shoppers and rotate them so they never visit the same shop twice in a six-month period.

A typical working day for a mystery shopper involves visiting stores, making purchases, and filing reports on various aspects of the visits. The mystery shoppers are employed on a part-time self-employed basis and receive a daily or hourly fee, depending on the assignment itself and the shopper's working experience. They are reimbursed for purchases and travel expenses, and compensated for car depreciation. An extra perk is that mystery shoppers are often permitted to keep the products they bought.

Janet commented, "I enjoy the work and it suits me just fine as a single mum with two kids. But what I find really satisfying is when I see standards improving in stores. That makes my job really worthwhile, and I feel I'm making a contribution."

2. You work as a mystery shopper for Shopper Marketing Experts. Visit a local supermarket or store and assess it. Aspects of this assessment could include:

- appearance, organisation, and cleanliness
- staff appearance
- service: staff engagement and product knowledge
- visual merchandising: window, in-store and POS (point of sale) displays, posters, signage
- product samples
- store layout
- product mix and stock

3. Write a business report on your findings for Shopper Marketing Experts. Use this structure:

Introduction: Give the background and purpose of the assignment and an outlook to the upcoming structure of the report.

Body: Use headings and sub-headings to show the contents of each section. Include information on your method(s) of data collection, your findings, and any necessary discussion of your findings.

Conclusion: State the major conclusions and deductions that can be drawn from the body content.

H Pitch Presentation

You work as an account manager for Shopper Marketing Experts. Present your findings from Exercise G2 to the retailer – your client – and make suggestions for improvements. Try to convince your client to carry out these improvements.

PITCHING TIPS

Tell a real customer story using a real name and outlining the challenges facing that customer. Avoid giving too many details, statistics and plans. Trying to remember too much content and putting pressure on yourself will make you more nervous.

Relax – less really can be more. Use your pitch to prioritise the most important aspects. Don't overload your listeners but keep them engaged and involved, rather than letting them drown in nitty gritty detail. Further detail can always be given in a handout to the pitch that your client can read and consult at a later date.

Prepare both presentation slides and customer documentation so that you demonstrate that you understand how each tool is used in communication. This will appear more professional and create a better impression.

WORD BANK: PROMOTION

buying allowance: A price discount given by a manufacturer to wholesalers and retailers to encourage them to buy a product or larger quantity of a product, so that the wholesalers and retailers are more likely to promote the product.

cooling off period: A period of time after a sales contract is agreed during which the buyer can cancel or withdraw from the contract without paying any penalty.

dangler: A shelf sign that sways when the consumer walks past it.

economy pack: A pack that includes several products in a wrap that is cheaper than buying the product individually.

end aisle display / endcap: Display of product or merchandise located at the end of a row of shelving in a store or shop that calls attention to a special offer.

hard sell: Pressuring a consumer to buy a product or service by using forceful or aggressive advertising or language without giving the consumer time to weigh up his or her options.

impulse purchase or **impulse buy**: Consumer purchase of a product in a shop or store with little or no prior decision or research.

incentive: Money, premiums, or prizes that are given by a seller to motivate consumers to buy products or services.

in-pack premium: A gift placed inside the product packaging to encourage the consumer to purchase the product.

loss leader: A product is sold below cost or the profit margin to stimulate (lead to) sales of other products; e.g., an electronics store that sells CDs below cost to attract customers and sell music equipment. Can be used as a verb: "to loss lead".

necker: A coupon placed on the neck of a bottle.

on-pack offer: An offer made on packaging.

to oversell: To sell more of a product or service than can actually be supplied; or to emphasise good points excessively; e.g., Human Resources gave him the feedback that he oversold himself and therefore didn't get the job.

on-pack premium: A gift attached to a product or the product packaging used to influence the consumer to purchase the product.

premium: A low-cost item given free to the consumer as a condition of purchase; e.g., Domos gave a free Mr Super Clean keyring to everyone who bought an XXL package of CleanIT!. Laws on premiums can vary from country to country.

promotional allowance: A cash payment or discount given by the manufacturer to wholesalers or retailers to advertise or carry out promotions.

promotional tie-in: A sales promotion arrangement between retailers or manufacturers; e.g., WashPool recommends Bright White washing powder for use in its washing machines.

pull strategies: Tactics that "pull" the consumer towards the brand: -e.g. Domos runs a competition with a car as a prize that consumers can enter on purchasing CleanIT!. The strategy attracts the consumer to the brand rather than to the retailer. If the consumer wants the product, the retailer will stock it.

push strategies: Tactics that "push" the product into the distribution network using buying allowances, advertising allowances, sales promotion allowances, slotting allowances, and other incentives; e.g., Domos exhibiting at the Discovery NY trade fair, or the consumer spotting a prominent display of CleanIT! on the supermarket shelf at eye level (see slotting allowance) and making an instant decision to purchase, dropping a bottle of CleanIT! into the shopping trolley.

shelf talker: A cardboard, plastic, or paper advertisement of a product attached to the shelf to call the buyer's attention to the product.

shelf wobbler: A shelf talker that jiggles from side to side – "wobbles".

slotting allowance: A fee paid by manufacturers to retailers to stock new products or to get better shelf space; e.g., Domos paid top supermarket chains to place CleanIT! at eye level on the supermarket shelves.

traffic builder: A promotional campaign or activity; for example, giving premiums, with the target of increasing the number of shoppers in a shopping area or mall.

5 GUERRILLA MARKETING

Introduction

The first use of the term *guerrilla marketing* is attributed to Jay Conrad Levinson in his book *Guerrilla Marketing*, written in 1984. Guerrilla marketing refers to guerrilla war, which is irregular military action that uses tactics such as ambush, raiding or sabotage. In the same way, guerrilla marketing concentrates on taking the consumer by surprise using unconventional marketing strategy. The focus is on being shocking, unique and clever to gain the maximum results from minimal resources.

Discuss these statements:

- "Guerrilla marketing is outdated today and can no longer be considered unconventional."
- "Only small businesses benefit from guerrilla marketing tactics."
- "If a big business uses guerrilla tactics, then it is not true guerrilla marketing."
- "Guerrilla marketing is too time-consuming and can actually be expensive."
- "Guerrilla marketing has the potential to backfire, creating negative feelings about a company, brand, or product."

A Vocabulary

1. Match the type of guerrilla marketing (1-8) with the correct definition (a-h):

1. wild posting
2. ambient advertising
3. street marketing
4. ambush marketing

5. viral marketing
6. influencer marketing
7. stealth marketing
8. projection advertising

a. ____ Passing on a marketing message from person to person, creating growth in exposure and influence so that the message spreads like a virus.

b. ____ Placement of advertisements on unusual items or in unusual places where they would not be normally seen – escalators, park benches, etc. – sometimes called "out of home".

c. ____ Focusing on key leaders or individuals rather the whole target market, so that these leaders or individuals drive the message to the wider market.

d. ____ Placement of projected advertising still images or film onto a building without permission from the city or owner of the building.

e. ____ Associating product with an event in the minds of potential customers without the advertiser paying sponsorship expenses for the event.

f. ____ A marketing strategy that advertises a product to people without them knowing they are being marketed to, which can be considered unethical as there is no opportunity to opt out – includes product placement, use of an agent without revealing the sponsor behind an action (covert agent), etc.

g. ____ Targeted placement of posters without permission around city locations in order to advertise and create engagement and social media shares.

h. ____ Promotion of products or services in public places such as streets to directly connect with the customer and create interaction.

2 Circle the correct word in parentheses to complete the sentences.

a. Tone™ utilised the connective power of top vloggers to transform the start up company into one of the hottest brands. This is an example of (ambush marketing/stealth marketing/influencer marketing).

b. I.M. Vile released his new album, *Contagious*, and in a (projection advertising/wild posting/viral marketing) campaign, Contagious posters appeared on unauthorised locations across building sites and underpasses nationwide.

c. Blue Cow decided on (wild posting/street marketing/ambient advertising) and employed street team members who drove a Blue Cow van and dressed up as blue cows. They acted as brand ambassadors and hit the streets to hand out products and engage with customers.

d. In a (viral marketing/stealth marketing/wild posting) campaign, *The Low Down on Celebrity Dirt* film had 3 million views within the first month and was shared across social media.

e. It was the 100th birthday of the famous Arcade building. Giant Burger captured the moment by using (ambient advertising/ambush marketing/projection advertising). When the sun went down and day turned to night, visitors saw a huge Giant Burger projected onto the building.

f. Strongarm placed oversized bottles with the distinctive Strongarm shape on well known statues and monuments in major cities as commuters were leaving work on a Friday afternoon. Commuters photographed these unusual sights of Strongarm and shared their photos on social media. Strongarm has used (ambient advertising/influencer marketing/ambush marketing).

g. Actors worked as covert agents and went to coffee bars and restaurants. In this (projection advertising/ambient advertising/stealth marketing) action, these actors ordered Blue Cow energy drink, which they then recommended to other customers.

h. Core Computers was the official sponsor of the football tournament. Their competitor, Maxi Computers, used (ambush marketing/viral marketing/street marketing). At the final game of the tournament, Maxi Computers gave T-shirts in the team colours with a distinctive Maxi logo to everyone seated behind the goal. The world's cameras zoomed in every time there was play in the penalty area focusing on the mass of Maxi logo T-shirts.

3. Find 3 examples of each type of guerrilla marketing activity (1-8) or a report about each marketing activity online. Evaluate each activity:

- Does the activity grab your attention? Why / Why not?
- Do you find the activity: imaginative, creative, fun, memorable? Why / Why not?
- Is the activity risky and/or innovative?
- Is the guerrilla marketing activity the right choice or fit for that brand?

B Guerrilla Marketing: Case Study

1. Read the case study about Tone below. Then give definitions for words or expressions from the text in bold.

a. cut-throat competition =   d. brand conscious =

b. challenger brand =   e. word of mouth =

c. lifestyle brand =   f. buzz =

TONE™

Four major players dominate the washing powder market in the UK, and there is **cut-throat competition** between these market leaders. All four players hold a portfolio of household name brands and observe each other constantly in order to gain a competitive edge and keep on a close eye on product reformulations, packaging innovations, acquisitions and marketing activities.

The category is one where marketing an innovation or a unique selling proposition is problematic, as research has shown that consumers fundamentally believe that washing powder is simply washing powder and that there is actually little difference between the products behind brands. Consumers do not frequently switch washing powder brands because they are sceptical about product innovation and tend to stick to brands they know. They sometimes buy private labels in times of economic downturn. However, one of the four major players, Domos, did manage to gain a step against its rivals with its generic advertising campaign *The World Needs Clean* two years ago.

What the four major players failed to do, though, was to reassess the structure of the market and identify market niches, which presented Tone™ with a gap to enter the market. This **challenger brand** was developed by three friends who met at university through their love of sport and fitness activities. They spotted that people who do a lot of sport also have a lot of washing and that sport clothes are usually mixed with other clothes in the washing basket. Those who make sport a lifestyle choice spend enormous sums on branded sportswear and specialist sports kit. The friends believed that such sports clothing should be washed separately with as much care as silk or other delicate fabrics but with a product that was strong enough to wash off sweat and dirt. Tone™ was born.

Tone™ was not introduced as another washing powder but as a **lifestyle brand**, marketed under the slogan *Raise the Tone,* targeting people who want to be fit and healthy and are **brand conscious**. Consumers could remain loyal to traditional washing powder brands but buy an additional upmarket product specifically for sportswear. At first, Tone™ was not introduced into supermarkets but only distributed through a small number of exclusive fitness clubs. Sales took off.

When it came to expansion, the friends unanimously agreed that they did not want to use expensive mass media TV, print, and radio advertising. Tone™ was selling due to **word of mouth** and the **buzz** that was slowly but steadily being created around the brand. It was cool, cheeky and unconventional, and could take a risk. The founders felt that Impetus, a boutique advertising agency specialising in guerrilla marketing, was exactly the right fit for the brand.

Impetus devised a wild posting campaign using the *Raise the Tone* slogan, which was printed in a bold typeface on posters in neon blue, green, and yellow tones. The agency targeted city areas that were in need of regeneration, particularly sports and playing areas, posting multiple posters in striking colourful displays. Photographs of the displays in various cities were shared across social media and prompted some local authorities to start urban regeneration programmes creating further positive buzz around the Tone™ brand.

At the same time, a number of communities contacted Tone™ for permission to start their own sports and playing field regeneration schemes using the *Raise the Tone* slogan and theme. Tone™ embraced these programmes and sponsored activities using them to distribute free product samples and *Raise the Tone* giveaways. Communities began to film their local events and post them on social media, encouraging citizens to take pride in their local city environment and to give time and energy to developing innovative schemes. *Raise the Tone* became a media buzzword. The brand got further publicity and crossed over to mass media with minimum expense when newspapers and radio and TV channels ran news items on the *Raise the Tone* phenomenon.

The four major players have recognised the rapid growth of Tone™ and have begun to look at niche sectors themselves. They probably won't target the sportswear niche because the Tone™ brand has firmly established itself as *the* brand here and is tough to challenge. Some commentators believe that one of the major players may try to acquire the Tone™ brand as an alternative strategy.

2. Discuss the questions.

- How did wild posting match the Tone™ brand?
- Could you suggest other guerrilla marketing types that Impetus could have used?
- If you were an owner of the Tone™ brand, would you sell your brand to one of the four market leaders?

C Viral Marketing: Case Study

1. Read the *TrapIT!* case study.

TrapIT!

In the 1980s, Domos began one of the most dramatic periods of growth in its history as it began to step up its internationalisation strategy on the road to globalisation. Domos had been known as a producer of cleansing products for decades, but it expanded by first acquiring the Curatio Health Group and then by establishing a new division to develop a product range for cleaning appliances.

The cleaning appliances division was given a free hand to develop innovative products, although the division was instructed to also uphold Domos' core values: *Honest*, as Domos products deliver on promises; *Fair*, as Domos products are high quality that are good value for money; *Uncompromising*, as Domos never stops striving to be the market leader; and *Proud*, as Domos stands for quality and pride in the home.

TrapIT! was introduced to the market in the late 1990s as a revolutionary new mopping system. Its USP (Unique Selling Proposition) was that it broke up and then trapped dirt, leaving floors shining and clean. TrapIT! got the best results when used together with Domos' cleaning product, CleanIT! Today, TrapIT! is lightweight, high tech, and available in a range of modern trendy colours with models for different types of flooring. The product has a high technology focus and is a lifestyle choice for modern households. It is sold in the upmarket price segment.

The current positioning is a result of market research first conducted in 2010, after which a strategy was developed to push consumers to engage emotionally with the TrapIT! brand. The marketing strategy aimed to get people excited about a household cleaning appliance, gain maximum exposure, and create a sense of "cool" about the brand. It was hoped that loyal customers would become advocates who would recommend the brand to others.

Domos used both above the line and below the line promotion to achieve these goals. ATL activities included television advertisements for raising awareness, press advertising, and billboards at selected locations. The advertising emphasised the USP and the core values. BTL included direct emails sent to customers, linking the message to the online shop. The product was demonstrated at exhibitions, giving both retailers and consumers the opportunity to see and touch the products. Point of sale materials were supplied to retailers, and promotions were offered to both retailers and consumers. Domos' website shared material such as brand photography and press releases so that retailers could use this material in their own promotions. PR included press releases, blogs and social media.

An essential part of the brand positioning was the development of a viral marketing campaign called Low Down on Celebrity Dirt. A film commissioned by Domos and posted online was at the centre of this campaign. This "documentary" showed a number of famous people trying to hide their "dirt" in a humorous and ironic style. The celebrities were stars who were particularly popular with young target groups.

Domos wanted to emphasise the coolness of its brand and produce a film that entertained rather than advertised. Although the film was based around TrapIT!, it did not mention the brand directly. The documentary style of the film aimed to get consumers talking and thinking about the brand differently. One of the celebrities in the film had set up a blog the previous year, and this back-story created anticipation in the build-up to the event.

The film caught the imagination of millions of viewers in an extremely short period of time when viewers shared the film on social media. It was discussed on blogs and shared across social media platforms, exposing TrapIT! to a global audience. Both press and TV ran news stories on the phenomenon.

Estimates conclude that the Low Down on Celebrity Dirt viral marketing campaign gave Domos at least a tenfold return on investment (ROI), helping Domos change consumer perceptions of the TrapIT! brand and reaching a worldwide audience. It also provided Domos with the potential to build on the campaign through other promotional activities.

2. Discuss the questions.

- Did TrapIT! match Domos' core values?
- What did the market research reveal in 2010?
- Was the combined ATL and BTL strategy the correct one for the brand?
- What was the content of "Low Down on Celebrity Dirt"?
- Should marketing entertain?
- Should marketing be kept fresh and new?

D Pitch Presentation

1. Domos has developed three innovative products and believes a viral campaign best suits the launch of each one.

Choose one of the following products and design a campaign:

- a. A household cleaner that has the fragrance of freshly baked bread
- b. A fabric softener with exciting new fragrances in a handy spray can for daily use
- c. An air freshener for households with babies and toddlers

Viral Marketing Tips

Make it viral!

That's a demand that's easy for your client to make.

Viral's cheap, but a viral campaign is also unpredictable. Here are some key concepts that can help you create your next viral campaign:
- Aim to be humourous, informative, surprising, remarkable, funny, outrageous, unique, controversial, courageous, crazy and/or entertaining
- Include an emotional hook
- Give a clear message
- Match the brand
- Tell a story
- Give people a stake in sharing your content.

www.viral-it.com

2. Pitch your ideas to Domos, explaining how the campaign fits the brand and how and why it will go viral.

PITCHING TIPS

Communicate with every single member of the audience by addressing all channels of communication, different language preferences, and learning types.

Story telling gives you a great chance to do this:
Visual – "See the blue sky and the red roses"
Auditory – "Hear the bees buzzing"
Kinaesthetic – "Feel the warmth of the sun"
Olfactory – "Smell the roses"
Gustatory – "Taste the delicious honey produced by the bees"

E Media Planning

1. Read the information about the role of the media planner and the media buyer.

The **media planner** is responsible for adjusting media schedules and monitoring the effectiveness of chosen media. S/he has research skills and responsibilities that include knowing the target audience and the media that can best access that target audience.

The **media buyer** should have good negotiating skills because s/he is in charge of getting the best media rates and managing the budget. Both the planner and the buyer liaise with clients and creatives.

Media planning and buying can be combined in one role.

2. Each medium has advantages and disadvantages when placing advertisements. What are some of the advantages and disadvantages of utilising these media for placing advertisements? Use the ideas in the chart below, and discuss with a partner or group.

- print (e.g., newspapers and magazines)
- radio
- TV
- direct mail
- outdoor
- ambient
- Internet
- social media

ADVANTAGES	DISADVANTAGES
• is cheap • is targeted • has high frequency • has a long history • allows use of the imagination • allows for a rapid response • combines sound and visual elements • is convenient • has credibility • can be spread by word of mouth • is interactive • has low production costs • is measurable • has high visibility • is good for demonstration • is modern • generates buzz • reaches a secondary audience • has global reach • allows some segmentation • allows explanation of complex issues • is fashionable • advertising is expected • is portable • is a platform for dialogue with the consumer	• has a limited time to communicate the message • has a short shelf life • is inflexible • is subject to zapping (using the TV remote to change TV channels) • is subject to zipping (fast forwarding of recorded TV, particularly through commercial breaks) • is ubiquitous • lacks a visual element • lacks impact • is "wallpaper" to other activities (= a background activity) • is limited by data protection laws • lacks control and / or interactivity • needs a high rate of repetition • leads to copyright issues • makes measurement of ROI difficult • generates the possibility of consumers' negative comments • has low reach • needs a good location to be effective • is a short-term fad • consistency of message is difficult to achieve

WORD BANK: GUERRILLA MARKETING

astroturfing: Employees or sponsors attempt to create the impression of widespread grassroots support for a product or service using forums, blogs etc. and may write under a pseudonym.

cost per rating point – CPP: Cost per 1% of a specified audience of buying advertising space in a given medium

cost per thousand – CPM: Cost per 1000 people reached of buying advertising space in a given medium.

coverage: Measuring reach of a medium within a specific geographic area.

early adopters: Early customers of new products, companies, and technologies who have influence over other consumers and advertise via word of mouth. Also called "lighthouse customers".

flash mob: A large group of people who assemble suddenly in a public place, perform and then quickly disperse.

lightbulb moment: A sudden moment of inspiration; e.g., Impetus had a lightbulb moment and created the *Raise the Tone* campaign.

marketing clutter: Volume of marketing messages the average consumer is exposed to on a daily basis.

media plan: A scheme giving objectives, strategy, budget, and media schedule and mix to reach a targeted audience.

media strategy: A plan of action for bringing advertising messages to the attention of consumers through the use of appropriate media.

millennial marketing: Marketing to people born between roughly 1980 and 2000 as one demographic, who grew up with technology, the Internet, and social media.

rating point: 1% of households who view a particular TV station at a given time or 1% of listeners who listen to a particular radio station at a given time.

stunt marketing: Releasing humourous or false breaking news for PR, media coverage, and public attention.

touchpoint: The place where a customer comes into contact with a brand; e.g. direct mail, website, online customer review, etc.

WOM: word of mouth.

6 CORPORATE IDENTITY

Introduction

Corporate identity is the physical portrayal of a company to the external world. This is in the control of the company, which determines the signals it gives. Corporate identity is conveyed by visual identity (e.g., corporate colours), marketing communications, corporate communications, employee behaviour (e.g., customer interaction), etc.

Corporate image is the perception of a company by the market and the impression given to stakeholders and the public. The image reflects the company's approach to business, its values, product quality, management, leadership, and communication strategies. Corporate image is fluid, meaning that it can change overnight, sometimes for reasons outside of the company's control.

Discuss these statements:

- "Even small companies need to seriously consider the issues surrounding corporate identity."
- "If the corporate identity is consistent, the customer will also feel the product quality is consistent."
- "Corporate identity cannot be static and needs to be continually refreshed."
- "Corporate image begins with the managers who should set an example."
- "A good corporate image can take years to build and moments to destroy."
- "Companies run programmes to show they are socially responsible simply to increase business and not because they are genuinely interested in social responsibility."

A Corporate Identity (CI)

1. Read the introduction to the *Domos Style Manual* below and then answer the questions.

According to the text:

- What are elements of corporate identity?
- What are the aims of corporate identity?
- What protects corporate identity?

Domos Style Manual

This manual seeks to ensure a coherent identity for Domos on a worldwide basis to provide meaningful symbols for global stakeholders. The Domos name and visual identity encapsulate our phi losophy, values and ethos, and are valuable assets fully protected by intellectual property (IP) laws guarding against infringement and copying.

Our new look is dynamic, fresh, and contemporary, but at the same time underlines Domos' heritage and quality.

The following pages contain guidelines on:
- logo, colours, typefaces and imagery, including use for stationery, websites, signage, livery, clothing, and buildings
- communication in Domos tone of voice
- usage of trademarks for premiums, POS materials and the media.

Correctness and consistency are key. Inconsistency weakens the Domos brand and dilutes the message Domos presents to the outside world.

2. Find three identity style guides for companies or brands online. Analyse and compare the contents.

3. Pitch Presentation: You work for an agency specialising in brand and corporate identity.
- Develop elements of the new CI for Domos.
- Pitch your concepts to the Domos management board.

PITCHING TIPS

Focus on the core ideas. You've chosen a stunning shade of red for the logo, and you know its colour codes. But why is this red the best colour for the message your client wants to give to the world? Don't teach your client about how your business works, but explain benefits and outcomes.

Timing is important. You are pitching to the management board, whose time is limited. Again, focus. Demonstrate that you have read the client's brief, understand it completely, and can contribute to growing the client's business.

This is a competitive pitch presentation to win lucrative business. Decide exactly what makes you different from other agencies and incorporate this in your pitch.

4. Congratulations! You have won the pitch to Domos. Now carry out these tasks.
   a. Brainstorm three words that encapsulate Domos (e.g., fun/playful/light-hearted; conservative/serious/formal; multicultural/diverse/aware.).
   b. Domos aims to ensure consistency of tone of voice in communications. Bearing your three words in mind, write:
      1. The "About Us" page for a national Domos website
      2. An article or a social media platform (length: about one A4 page)
      3. A blog post about the history of a Domos brand. (length: about one A4 page)

B Corporate Image

1. Choose a well-known company from each of these industrial sectors:

- banking
- technology
- healthcare

What is the corporate image of each company? Use words from the chart below and your own ideas.

Positive Attributes	Negative Attributes	General Attributes
accountable	confused	conservative
agile	secretive	cool
caring	uncaring	creative
customer focused	unethical	diverse
dedicated	unfriendly	evolving
dynamic	inflexible	family focused
ethical	unrealistic	formal
exciting	unreliable	informal
flexible	untrustworthy	liberal
friendly		multifaceted
innovative		sophisticated
inspirational		specialised
reliable		unique
transparent		
trustworthy		
visionary		
vibrant		

2. Discuss these questions.

- Why does each of these companies have this corporate image?
- What constant actions can a company take to improve its corporate image?
- What are some of the reasons corporate image might change?
- What actions can a company take to repair damage to its corporate image?

C Corporate Image Film

1. Read this briefing for Domos.

BRIEFING

Project
Domos has just signed a ten-year deal to sponsor the Constantia Games.

The Constantia Games is an alternative annual event for athletes with a wide range of physical disabilities. Constantia's mission is to celebrate life and those with the determination and strength to succeed when life has not dealt them the fairest playing hand. Constantia reflects Domos' core values: honest, fair, uncompromising, and proud.

Domos plans to make a 30-minute pilot documentary film to publicise our new relationship with Constantia to promote Domos' corporate image. It will be posted on social media and also used at corporate events and presentations.

Target Audience
The film is targeted at young and old. It should be contemporary but also corporate. We are looking for a creative approach that can combine these elements.

Tone
- Inspirational
- Motivating
- Determined
- Uncompromising
- Never Say Die attitude
- The Will to Win

Style
Professional with high production values.

Future Prospects
Depending on the success of the pilot project film, a budget can be allocated to producing a series of films over the ten-year period of the sponsorship.

> **Production values**: The quality of a media production, such as a film, with regard to style, quality, colours, etc.

2. In small groups, create the outline of this corporate image film as Domos' agency, using a basic storyboard to outline the scenes and storyline.

3. Present this outline to Domos, highlighting the PR benefits for Domos. Explain why and how this film will be shared on social media.

D Crisis Management

> A **corporate crisis** can evolve from a wide range of internal and external circumstances, and can damage or enhance corporate identity, depending on the company's management of the crisis. Examples of crisis scenarios are natural disasters, protests, technological problems, employee misconduct, environmental catastrophe, or a national emergency.

1. Read the guidelines in the text *Crisis? What Crisis?* Do you agree with them?

Crisis? What Crisis?

Crises can come from unlikely directions and be unpredictable. The response can be more critical than the incident itself. Here are some guidelines:
- Prepare your team. Create a Crisis Management Team (CMT). Give members of the team clearly defined roles and responsibilities, and practise for a crisis. Ensure that external and internal contact details are recorded. Nominate a spokesperson and ensure s/he gets media training.

- Prepare by building a good reputation and good relationships with the media. Develop professional social media management. These will provide rock-solid foundations when a crisis hits.
- Take decisive action. Be proactive and react speedily. Don't speculate. Get the facts, but use fast and effective communication at the same time.
- Accept responsibility. Admit you have made a mistake or are in the wrong when you know this is the case. Denial can be costly. Be honest and truthful. Apologise when you really need to.
- Take a stand. Don't be wishy-washy. Maybe, you are not in the wrong; but state this clearly and publicly.
- Respond to media enquiries. Ensure accurate media coverage by ensuring the media has your position and point of view, and not only those from other sources.
- Communicate with all stakeholders.
- Be human. Drop the corporate face and jargon and connect on a human level. A sense of humour goes a long way in the right situation.
- Be systematic. Engage with different parts of your organisation and external bodies as necessary.
- Be flexible and adaptable. Every crisis is different. Adapt so that you can respond more effectively and efficiently.
- Evaluate after the crisis. Assess what went well and what went badly. Record the evaluation for future planning.

2. Read the two following case studies: *Domos Tablets* and *Giant Burger Firing*. Evaluate the crisis management in each case. Use the chart below to take notes for your discussion.

Evaluation Criteria	Domos	Giant Burger
Preparation		
Media relations		
Social media management		
Speed of reaction		
Acceptance of responsibility		
Communication		
Adaptability		
Damage to corporate image		

Domos Tablets

In 1998, Domos introduced a new washing powder in the form of a blue and red tablet. The company believed it had a revolutionary innovation that meant that washing powder could be delivered in smaller packages that were both easier to transport and better for the environment. The product was launched with a massive nationwide ATL campaign.

A problem quickly arose. It turned out that small children sometimes mistook the blue and red tablets for sweets, and many children were taken to accident and emergency departments with stomach complaints. The complaints were not life-threatening, but the symptoms were extremely unpleasant and very distressing for parents. The company began to receive letters from both doctors and parents.

Domos had made a huge investment in the new product, and sales had rocketed in the first months after the launch. However, the company acknowledged it had an unexpected problem and decided to react immediately by issuing a press release and holding a press conference to outline details of the customers' complaints. The CEO apologised and warned parents that they should place the tablets out of reach of children. At the same time, Domos announced a product recall and told parents that they could return any purchase of the tablets to their local store to get a full refund and a voucher for free Domos products as an apology. The company got to work on developing new packaging and introduced its "child-lock" packaging two months later.

Domos never disclosed information about its short-term financial losses. However, it managed to save its product for the long term by being proactive and taking swift action. Domos admitted it had made a mistake and corrected it. Today, tablets are the washing product of choice for 35% of households. Advertising still mentions that Domos is trustworthy and truly addresses public safety issues.

Giant Burger Firing

In 2015, Giant Burger fired an employee at one of its restaurant in Wellington, New Zealand. What did he do? Keith Lester posted photographs of his workplace on his page on a well-known social media platform. The photographs depicted a restaurant that fell well below the cleanliness and corporate identity guidelines set by Giant Burger headquarters in New York. Lester was fired for violating company policy, although Giant Burger regularly posts photos of its worldwide restaurants on its social media accounts.

News of the firing spread like wildfire across all social media platforms. People generally felt that Lester was not responsible for the fundamental management problems at the Wellington restaurant and that his case had been handled insensitively by New York.

Giant Burger responded with a detailed blog defending their actions. This quickly drew over 100,000 negative comments worldwide. Giant Burger added fuel to the fire by not making individual responses but repeatedly posting the same company statement in reply to comments. The company also deleted some negative comments and blocked users at the same time. It continued to persist in defending its actions and even argued with users who criticised the restaurant chain. By the next day, the original Giant Burger blog had generated over 300,000 comments and attracted mass media attention.

E Press Conference

1. Role play a press conference with Domos, the Domos press conference support team, and the media. First, read the following email from the CEO at Domos to all employees.

From: Ivor Goody <imf0088@xxxxxxx.com.tw>
Date: Fri, Jan 31, 20XX at 11:57 AM
Subject: Accusations about nails in Magic Soft packaging

Dear employees at Domos,

At the beginning of last week, a customer posted photographs of nails that she had allegedly found in a bottle of Magic Soft fabric softener. She went on to make several claims, stating that her young children could have been badly hurt and her washing machine had been irreparably damaged. The photos were shared across social media, and our customer services department had received more than 100 reports of similar cases and claims for compensation from across the country by last Friday.

We were absolutely confident that these claims were false and that our manufacturing processes were not at fault. Nevertheless, we immediately checked all processes thoroughly. In addition, two large supermarket chains supplied us with CCTV footage showing shoppers tampering with packaging and putting nails into the opaque plastic bottles used to package Magic Soft. At this point, we contacted the police, who are conducting their own criminal investigation. Today, the woman who posted the original photos admitted she fabricated her claims and is being questioned by police.

We are holding a press conference tomorrow morning. Reporters from major TV channels and radio stations as well as editors from major newspapers will be attending. All claims against the company will be refuted, and Domos intends to once again prove that we are completely honest and trustworthy. We will in fact "hit the nail on the head!"

In the meantime, let me take this opportunity to thank you all for your continuing loyalty and the pride you have consistently demonstrated in working for Domos.

Thank you,
Ivor Goody
CEO

2. Divide into three groups (A, B, and C) of 2-8 people to role play the press conference.

Group A: Domos

- Choose a Media Relations Manager, the moderator at the press conference. His /Her role is to welcome participants, introduce members of the panel from the company to the media, follow the agenda, direct questions from the media to the correct member of the Domos panel, make a short summary at the end of the conference, and thank journalists and editors for coming.
- All other Group A participants are spokespeople for Domos. Decide who has what role: CEO, Director of Production, Director of Corporate Communications, worker from the production line of Magic Soft, Director of Customer Services and/or anyone else you feel is appropriate. Each participant prepares a 3-minute presentation examining one aspect of the crisis.

- As a group, decide on an agenda. Rehearse and ensure everyone involved is giving a consistent message. You may wish to include some video footage to underline your case.
- •repare a list of ten questions you anticipate being asked but would find difficult to answer. Decide who is responsible for answering which question. Rehearse answering these questions.

Group B: Domos press conference support team

1. Prepare the room for the conference.
2. Prepare a press release to be included in a media kit given to journalists and editors at the conference.
3. Welcome participants from the media as they arrive and sign them in.
4. Observe the press conference and prepare to give feedback after the conference. Feedback includes comments on:
    - consistency of message
    - clarity of message given by spokespeople
    - the achievement of Domos' objectives
    - what went well
    - what could be improved
    - suggestions for future press conferences.
5. Give your feedback to Domos (Group A).

Group C: Media

1. Choose group members to represent TV channels, radio stations, or newspapers.
2. Each channel, station, or newspaper representative prepares a list of questions to ask during the press conference. Questions should be both friendly and hostile towards Domos. Rehearse asking these questions and try to anticipate possible answers.
3. At the press conference, each media representative introduces themselves before asking a question and asks any necessary follow up questions.
4. Each media representative writes a news article after the press conference.

WORD BANK: CORPORATE IDENTITY and CORPORATE IMAGE

Act of God: A legal term used in contracts and insurance policies – an event that occurs due to natural causes that could not have been prevented, e.g. an earthquake or a tsunami.

benchmark: A standard or a set of standards that are used to evaluate and measure performance, e.g. Domos used benchmarks to establish metrics for crisis management performance.

chain of command: The line of hierarchical authority in a company or a crisis management team.

CMP: Crisis Management Plan.

colour palette: The range of primary and secondary colours used in corporate or brand identity.

contingency plan: A plan devised for an outcome other than in the usual expected plan.

crisis containment: Limitation or restriction of the harmful consequences or threats from a crisis; e.g.,Domos contained the crisis by admitting its mistake and recalling its products.

typography: Typefaces used in corporate or brand identity, described with weights, styles, and applications for headings and titles, subheadings, body copy, etc.

7 MARKETING RESEARCH

Introduction

Marketers utilise marketing research processes, methods, and tools to systematically gather information and close the information gap between manufacturers or service providers and their customers and/or end consumers, so that marketing opportunities, problems, actions, and performance can be identified, defined, evaluated, and improved. *Marketing research* covers the 4 Ps of the marketing mix (product, price, place, promotion) and involves collecting data about consumer preferences, product preferences, advertising effectiveness, consumer satisfaction, consumer motivations, buying behaviour, etc; whereas *market research* is a subset of marketing research; it covers just 'place' in the marketing mix and involves identifying and measuring a market.

Discuss these statements:

- "Marketing research is vital if manufacturers want to understand market demands."
- "Marketing research is not an exact science."
- "Managers do not understand that marketing research presents the facts but does not solve the problems."
- "Marketing research takes so long that some results become invalid."
- "The field of marketing research is underestimated, and there is a great need for well-trained expert researchers and interviewers."

A Primary and Secondary Research

1. Read the definitions of primary and secondary research.

> **Primary research**: Data not yet published, collected from an original source with a specific objective in mind.
> **Secondary research**: Processing data already collected and available from other sources.

2. Write the words in the box into the appropriate column in the chart.

> original, current, desk, Internet, verified, websites, unique, blogs, survey, questionnaire, government reports, observation, newspapers, company accounts, interview

Primary research	Secondary research

3. Write _P_ if the following examples are examples of primary research. Write _S_ if the examples are examples of secondary research.

a. _____ Consulting an article "The Detergents Market Today" in the _Today_ newspaper from 2012.

b. _____ Completing a 10-minute customer satisfaction survey.

c. _____ Consulting CleanIT! sales figures from 2000-2010.

d. _____ Completing a questionnaire with a total of 25 questions about your cleaning routine.

e. _____ Collecting data from a random sample of the population.

f. _____ Consulting the Government Environment Report, Section 3.2, Detergents.

g. _____ Submitting a report entitled, "The Observation of Consumer Behaviour (city centre supermarkets)".

h. _____ Using the Domos Annual Report.

i. _____ Collecting feedback on shopping experiences on a consumer website - www.consumerfeedback.biz.

j. _____ Conducting in-depth interviews on cleaning routines and habits.

B Quantitative, Qualitative and Ethnographic Research

1. Read about different types of research.

Quantitative Research: Measurements, calculations, or statistical data with the results generally in a numerical form. Answers the question, _How many?_

Qualitative Research: Exploration of thoughts, feelings, actions, and the reasons behind these to find out about consumer behaviour. Answers the question, _Why?_

Ethnographic Research: Observation of consumers in their own environment / culture.

2. Check (√) whether the following are examples of _quantitative_, _qualitative_, or _ethnographic_ research.

example	quantitative	qualitative	ethnographic
a. In the past week, how many times have you seen the CleanIT! TV commercial? Never 1 2 3 4 5+			
b. Please keep a video diary when you clean your kitchen.			
c. Did you have a positive reaction to the commercial? Yes/No			
d. This study is based on the observation of cleaning staff at work in office buildings.			
e. Why did you change your household cleaning product?			

f. If you were to describe Mr Super Clean to a friend, which of these words would you use? *memorable, strong, warm-hearted, humourous, kind-hearted, irritating, childish, attention-getting.*			
g. What do you think of Mr Super Clean?			
h. Which of these statements best describes the way you shop: *I window shop / I shop mostly online / I research the product and then buy / I impulse buy.*			
i. Researchers went to Sweden to live in Swedish households and observe household cleaning habits and routines.			
j. Why did you buy Mr Super Clean merchandise?			

C Questioning

1. Read the definitions in the box. Then discuss with a partner when closed-ended questions are more useful and when open-ended questions are more useful. Give specific examples.

> **Closed-ended questions:** Designed so the respondent gives a one-word answer such as *yes* or *no*, or is given explicit options to choose from.
> **Open-ended questions:** Designed without predetermined responses and in a manner that gives the respondent the opportunity to express opinions freely.

2. Are the following words and expressions more related to closed-ended questions or open-ended questions? Complete the chart:

> multiple choice, unanticipated answer, unique answer, check box, freedom and space, exploratory, qualitative, quantifiable, percentages, in-depth, drop down box, unlimited response, demographic information, conclusive, complex explanation necessary, ranking, consumer behaviour information

Closed-ended Questions	Open-ended Questions

3. Write C if the following (a-t) are closed-end questions and O if they are open-ended questions:

a. _____ What are your reasons for buying CleanIT!?

b. _____ What does Mr Super Clean mean to you?

Environmentally friendly

| Totally Agree | Rather Agree | Neither Agree or Disagree | Rather Disagree | Totally Disagree |

Superhero

| Totally Agree | Rather Agree | Neither Agree or Disagree | Rather Disagree | Totally Disagree |

Cleanliness

| Totally Agree | Rather Agree | Neither Agree or Disagree | Rather Disagree | Totally Disagree |

c. _____ Are cleaning products?

good for the environment   *bad for the environment*

| Extremely | Very | Quite | Don't Know | Quite | Very | Extremely |

good value for money   *bad value for money*

| Extremely | Very | Quite | Don't Know | Quite | Very | Extremely |

d. _____ State your opinion of the quality of CleanIT!

e. _____ Why do you buy the Clean IT! brand?

f. _____ What age are you?

☐ 0-18
☐ 18-30
☐ 31-40
☐ 41-50
☐ 51-60
☐ 61 and above

g. _____ What do you think about Mr Super Clean?

h. _____ Do you buy CleanIT!?

Yes | No

i. _____ If the price of CleanIT! increased:

I would certainly buy it   1   2   3   4   5   I would certainly not buy it

j. _____ What is your opinion of Mr Super Clean?

Very Positive / Positive / Neutral / Negative / Very Negative

k. _____ Why do you use CleanIT! more than any other cleaning product?

l. _____ Have you cleaned in the last 24 hours?

Yes | No

m. _____ Tell me about your cleaning routines.

n. _____ Which of these cleaning product brands do you buy the most often?

o. _____ Do you think Mr Super Clean encourages children to care for the planet?

Yes | No | Don't Know

p. _____ Why do you think that?

q. _____ What is the colour of your kitchen floor?

White | Black | Brown | Grey | Other

r. _____ Finish this story: "Mr Super Clean enters the room..."

s. _____ How do you feel about environmental issues?

t. _____ Is your kitchen floor made of:

Laminate | Tiles | Wood | Other?

D Interpretation of Research

Select 2 television commercials and 2 print advertisements. Discuss with a partner or a group what needs, product data, category insights and/or consumer insights might have arisen from research before the advertising / advertising campaign was developed.

E Reading Text

1. Complete the following text *Tips: Market Research on a Small Budget* by writing the correct heading (a-f) for each paragraph (1-6):

   a. Get Online
   b. A Valuable Tool
   c. Focus and Evaluate
   d. Trust Yourself
   e. If It's Cheap, Then Take Advantage
   f. Research Design

Tips: Marketing Research on a Small Budget

1. _____
Although multinational corporations can spend many millions of pounds on research, smaller organisations are forced to evaluate market opportunities on significantly tighter budgets, which can affect both the quantity and the quality of the research. These companies should thus concentrate on research objectives and appreciate that research is not insight until it is interpreted. Consequently, it is advisable to limit the amount of data collection and zero in on good analysis of this data.

2. _____
Small businesses should remember that a huge amount of secondary data is available. This includes government statistics, local authority reports, newspaper articles and reports from trade associations and other organisations. In addition, some research tools are available online at little or no cost.

3. _____
It is essential to find out exactly who the primary customer is and to gain consumer insights. A start-up can use networks of friends and colleagues to gather research. Everyone likes to be asked for advice, and everyone has an opinion. Gaps in the markets can be discovered by asking the right questions, resonating with prospects, eliciting responses and avoiding interviewer bias. Interviewer bias occurs when the interviewer poses questions in a way that elicit preconceived responses leading to distorted research findings.

4. _____
Social media can also play an important role for smaller businesses and those seeking to grow. People love to give their opinion but don't want to feel they are being manipulated. So, it is not only about collecting lots of followers and likes but also about building engagement and brand advocates.

5. _____
It is not the most scientific method of research, but small businesses cannot dismiss gut instinct. Passion can drive a business further and make time to market shorter than simply identifying a gap in the market. The approach to research should change as the organisation grows as it looks to expand.

6._____

Paying close attention to customers can be critical too. Businesses can learn a lot by watching the market and listening to customers. By simply using observation, any small business should be able to change and adapt very quickly. There is really no substitute for good qualitative research because the business is having a dialogue with the people that it needs to attract.

2. Find words or expression in the text above that mean:

    a. Aims of the study that may concern the product, service, advertising campaign, or media (paragraph 1)

    b. Research instruments (paragraph 2)

    c. Partiality to certain views or opinions corrupting the data collection (paragraph 3)

    d. Appeal to potential customers (paragraph 3)

    e. Truths about the consumer based on needs, wants, beliefs, experience and behaviour (paragraph 3)

    f. Trigger answers (paragraph 3)

    g. People who pass on positive word of mouth messages about the brand (paragraph 4)

    h. The amount of time from the first concept of a product to its launch on the market (paragraph 5)

    i. Intuition prompting a feeling to react in a certain way that is not based on reason or logic (paragraph 5)

F In-depth Interview Role Play

> **In-depth interview:** An intensive interview with an individual or a small group of respondents to explore attitudes, behaviour, and perceptions.

1. Divide into three groups (A, B and C) and read the information.

> CleanIT! unveiled a new nationwide campaign at the beginning of this year that introduced a new slogan *Power to the Planet*. It was supported by outdoor, press, in-store, and digital promotions. The campaign also introduced the *Mr Super Clean* character to the market.

Group A: Agency with its client, Domos

1. Your research objectives are to explore behaviour, attitudes, and perceptions towards the household cleanser category, the *Power to the Planet* campaign, and the Mr Super Clean character in particular.

2. Prepare a script with a set of questions (opening, exploring, follow-up/probing, and closing questions).

3. Conduct the interview with interviewees from group B:
    - Include an introduction and a closing section
    - Omit questions or change direction if you think it is necessary
    - Use follow-up (probing) questions as necessary
    - Take notes

4. After the interview, write a short report summarising both the category insights and the consumer insights.

Group B: Interviewee(s)

1. Participate in the interview. You have no hidden agenda, and aim to be as open and honest as possible.

2. After the interview, collect the final short report from Group A, the agency, and the client (Domos).
3. Changing to the role of the advertising agency, use the report to produce a questionnaire (15-20 questions) that will be used in follow-up quantitative research.

Group C: Agency observers

1. Before the interview, consult Group A, check on the research objectives and collect a copy of the script of prepared questions.
2. Observe the interview and give feedback on these areas:
   - Relevance of questions
   - Quality of follow-up questions
   - Listening
   - Rapport
   - Interviewer bias
3. Give your feedback to Group A.

G Focus Group Role Play

> **Focus Group:** A small number of target consumers are brought together to discuss a campaign at a stage from concept to post-production usually in a facility that has recording equipment and/or an observation room with one-way mirrors.

1. Divide into three groups, A, B, and C. Read the information about the CleanIT! target market to prepare for a focus group. Note: The focus group should last a minimum of one hour.

Target Market – CleanIT!

The core target market is males and females from the ages of 8 to 15 and their parents. Parents are both current and prospective users of CleanIT! and include mixed race, same sex and single parent households to reflect CleanIT!'s place in a multicultural, tolerant , 21st century society. Children, teenagers and parents probably have their concerns or feel guilty about purchasing and using certain cleaning products. It is likely that children even chastise their parents about their purchasing behaviour.

Group A: Agency Research Team

You have invited a number of target consumers for CleanIT! to a focus group at your agency as part of your marketing research where you will present your first ideas for the CleanIT! campaign.

1. Before the focus group, define your research objectives.
2. Prepare a script with a set of relevant questions.
3. Lead the focus group:
   - Start with a warm-up session so that the consumers feel comfortable with the agency and the other members of the consumer group.
   - Conclude by thanking the consumers.

Group B: Target Consumers for CleanIT!

You have been invited to a focus group at an advertising agency in your city. You don't really know what to expect but are looking forward to meeting some new people and having a sociable afternoon.

1. Before the focus group, prepare different roles for each member of the focus group.
2. Consider and discuss your attitudes to the home, cleaning, and the environment.
3. Attend the focus group.

Group C: Agency Observers

1. Before the focus group, consult Group A, the agency research team. Check the objectives of the focus group and collect a copy of the script of prepared questions.
2. Observe the focus group and prepare to give feedback in these areas:
   - Relevance of questions
   - Relevance of follow-up questions
   - Group dynamics and rapport.
3. After the focus groups, write a short report that includes consumer insights and recommendations for both Domos and the agency.

WORD BANK: MARKETING RESEARCH

ad recall: Use of marketing research tools to measure recollection of an advertisement, giving insight into the memorable attributes of the advertisement.

baby boomers: The generation born after World War II in the period from 1946 to around 1964.

Customer Relationship Management (CRM): Creating a long-term relationship with customers to track information about activities and preferences.

data protection: International and national laws that protect data privacy.

demographics: Age, gender, income, marital status, etc.

dichotomous question: A question with just two possible answers, e.g. "Yes / No".

Generation X: The generation born after the baby boomers, from around 1964 to the early 1980s.

Generation Y: The generation born after Generation X between around 1980 to 2000 (also called **millennials**).

Generation Z: The generation born from just before 2000 onwards.

Likert scale: a scale that measures how respondents "Agree" or "Disagree" with a statement; e.g., How do you feel about this statement? *Mr Super Clean means "environmentally friendly."*

Totally Agree / Rather Agree / Neither Agree or Disagree / Rather Disagree / Totally Disagree

lifelogging: People who are the subject of research carry cameras to record events as they happen.

loaded question: A question that is formed in a manner that elicits a specific response.

market segmentation: Taking a market and dividing it into sections with measurable characteristics; e.g., demographics, to identify the target market.

ordinal scale: ranking; e.g., What is your opinion of Mr Super Clean?

Very Positive / Positive / Neutral / Negative / Very Negative

post testing: Testing after a campaign has run.

ratio scale: Ranking in a scale that has a definite zero; e.g., *What age are you?* 0-18 □ 18-30 □ 31-40 □ 41-50 □ 51-60 □ 61 and above □

test market: A small market that is used for testing.

test screening: Screening of a commercial to a sample audience before it is aired.

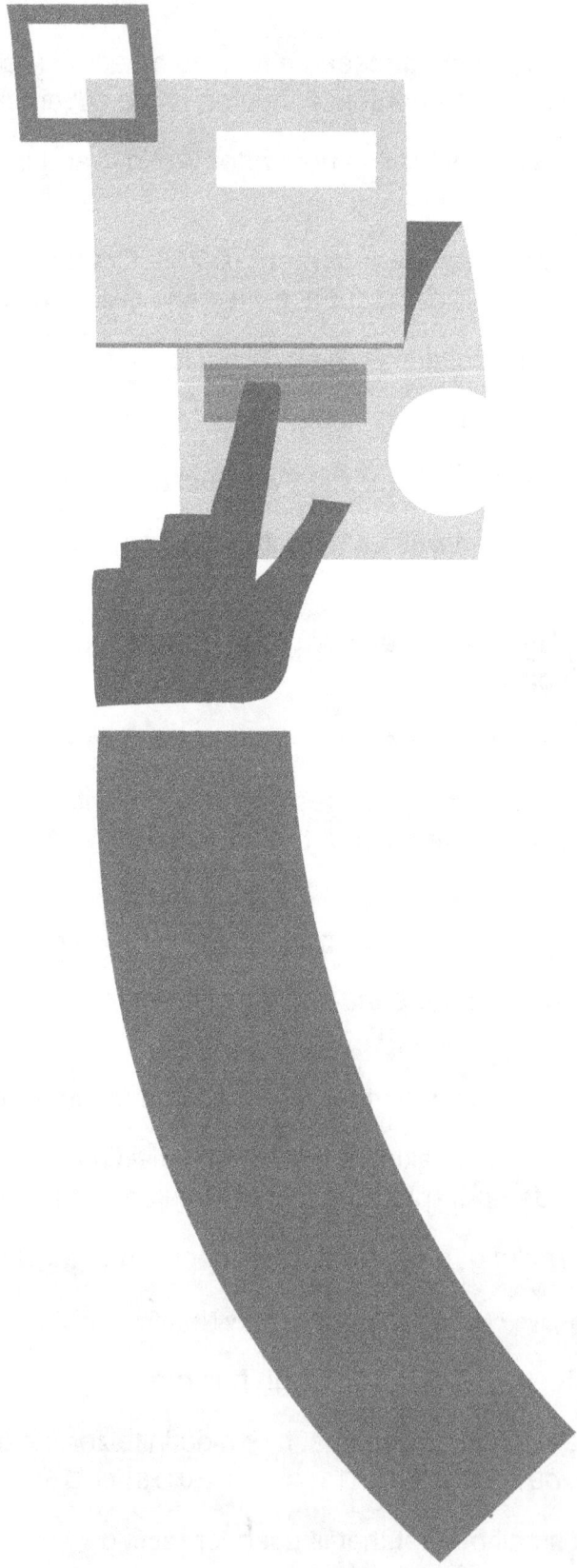

8 GLOBAL MARKETING

Introduction

Global marketing involves planning, producing, placing, and promoting products and services worldwide. The marketing mix that works in a domestic market may not be successful in other international markets, so the appropriate marketing mix must be decided on for various international markets. Global marketing communications involves considering culture, language, and other factors that differ from the domestic market.

1. Discuss the following questions with a partner:

    a. In terms of global marketing, define the differences between:
- an international company
- a multinational company
- a global company

    b. What factors should a company consider when doing business in a country outside its domestic market?

    c. From a marketing communications perspective, what are the issues if a company wants to deveop

    d. a domestic brand into a global brand?

    e. What are the values, beliefs, ideas, customs, actions and symbols of your country's culture that distinguish this culture?

    f. Choose another country and describe that country's culture.

    g. Are terms such as global citizen, global village and world economy just fashionable expressions, or are they applicable to business and marketing communications today?

    h. Identify elements that global brands have in common. Are there product categories that are better suited to a global marketing strategy?

    i. Is English the language of global marketing communications?

    j. What are the problems of translation in global marketing communications? How can these problems be overcome?

A Global Brands Ranking

1. Read the following text and examine the two rankings. Answer and discuss the questions that follow.

FxCom™ Brand Claims First Place

Xbrand, a corporate identity and brand consulting company, is responsible for Global Brand Ranking. On this year's ranking, the previous No. 1 brand, Big Fizz Soft Drinks, fell to No. 6. FxCom™ replaced Big Fizz Soft Drinks in first place, and Big Fizz was not in the top five in the ranking for the first time.

This year's report stated, "There are companies that enter the market and change our lives. This is why we have a new number one this year." The report estimates the value of the FxCom™ brand at $150 billion, up 35 percent from last year. The value of Big Fizz Soft Drinks brand has dropped by 11 percent to $75 billion in the last five years. A spokesperson for Big Fizz commented, "Nothing lasts forever. Delivering on brand promise remains our focus."

FxCom™ and other leading technology brands are today's high fliers. This is emphasised by the brand in second place, Faster Connect Technologies, which has soared from twentieth place last year. In fact, four of the top brands are technology brands. HeartStop is ranked as a services brand. Otherwise, technology would account for five of the top ten. However, not all technology brands performed well; Quick Connect Mobile Phones disappeared from this year's list; Wild West finished the year in 67th place.

Top Ten Global Brands 2005	Top Ten Global Brands Today
1. Big Fizz Soft Drinks (U.S.A.)	1. FxCom™ (U.S.A.: Internet services)
2. Giant Burger Fast Food Restaurants (U.S.A.)	2. Faster Connect Technologies (South Korea)
3. Quick Connect Mobile Phones (Finland)	3. Core Computers (U.S.A.)
4. Big Fry Fast Food Restaurants (U.S.A.)	4. Maxi Computers (U.S.A.)
5. Maxi Computers (U.S.A.)	5. Vision (U.S.A.: social media)
6. GMW (Germany: vehicles)	6. Big Fizz Soft Drinks (U.S.A.)
7. Wild West (U.S.A.: tobacco)	7. Vanon (Japan: vehicles)
8. Fantasy (U.S.A.: films, merchandising)	8. BMF (U.S.A.: consultancy and services)
9. BMF (U.S.A.: consultancy and services)	9. Giant Burger Fast Food Restaurants (U.S.A.)
10. Finesse (U.S.A.: vehicles)	10. HeartStop (U.S.A.: online entertainment)

2. Work with a partner. Take turns comparing the ranking in 2005 and the ranking today by completing these statements:

  a. Technology has developed since 2005. The changes I can see are ...
  b. I can identify lifestyle changes such as ...
  c. The country that had the most brands in the top ten in 2005 was the United States. Countries that have come into the top ten since 2005 are _____ and _____ This has happened because...
  d. Quick Connect Mobile Phones and GMW have disappeared from the current ranking of the top ten. This could be because ...

3. Which actual brands would you place in the current top ten of global brands?

  a. Check your list with a current ranking on the Internet. Does anything surprise you?
  b. How do you think the list was different 10 years ago?
  c. How do you think the list might be different in another 10 years?

d. Which companies would you place in the world's top ten? Check your list with a current list on the Internet. Compare this list with the brands' list. Can you explain the similarities and differences?

B Standardisation v. Adaptation

> A strategic decision is whether to use a standardised marketing mix and a single marketing strategy in all countries, or whether to adjust the marketing mix and strategies to fit and adapt to each local market.

1. The following comments are taken from the websites of global restaurant chains. Do the comments (1-12) match a standardisation or an adaptation strategy? Write S or A.

a._____ We deliver consistent restaurant experiences to all customers worldwide.

b._____ We do not sell beer in the Republic of Terra Firma as beer sales are illegal.

c._____ Our global core values are quality and cleanliness.

d._____ Our home slogan is in English, and it is translated into local equivalents.

e._____ Restaurants must adhere to the design and layout parameters established by the global headquarters.

f._____ Our advertisements are shot in 15 different languages featuring the customised products catering to each region.

g._____ Customers can expect the same level of quality and service anywhere around the world.

h._____ Due to religious restrictions, beef is not offered in India.

i._____ We include more chicken meals on the menu in China as chicken is more popular than beef.

j._____ We have been sponsors of global sporting events such as the Olympics and the World Cup for the past 30 years.

k._____ Part of the marketing budget is allocated to local promotions that are tailored to the local market.

l._____ We ensure that the same ethically sourced coffee is served in all restaurants worldwide.

C Bright White Adaptation: Case Study

1. Read the Bright White branding case study and answer the following questions with a partner.

a. What facts are given about the washing powder category?

b. Why did Fitch & Fitch believe the Friends campaign would probably be effective in the UK market?

c. What evidence is given for the lack of success in the UK market?

d. What evidence is given for the success of the Real Students campaign?

e. Is it possible to have a single global campaign or must campaigns always be adapted to the local market?

f. Do you know other campaigns that take a global idea that is adapted to different countries?

Bright White Adaptation

Domos is a global company with a portfolio of brands aimed at a range of different target groups. Bright White, a washing powder, is one of these brands, and was originally targeted at consumers between the ages of 25 and 35. Domos made the decision to target young people between the ages of 18 and 25 when these consumers buy washing powder for the first time after moving out of their parents' home. The vision was to make Bright White a global leader by establishing a relationship with young consumers that would lead to long-term loyalty.

The company employed Fitch & Fitch as their advertising agency in the United States. Fitch & Fitch developed the *Friends* campaign, featuring college students talking about how their life was made easier because they used Bright White. The idea had emerged from observing focus groups in which young people said they usually chose a washing powder recommended by their peers and not the one used by their parents.

The campaign was so successful in the US that it was adopted for the UK. However, Domos did not achieve its key objectives in the UK. Bright White did not become the most popular brand amongst young consumers, and it did not establish a connection with young consumers. Moreover, the future growth of the brand was threatened by competitors, who were increasingly targeting young consumers, and Bright White's positioning was in jeopardy. Why?

The advertising campaign lacked impact, did not help to generate empathy, and did not lead to increases in sales. Bright White's advertising awareness was low in comparison to competitors, and the ratio between advertising awareness and advertising spend was low. Research by Fitch & Fitch revealed the problem lay with the American advertising, which was viewed negatively by British consumers. *Friends* worked in the US but young people in the UK found the style and content of the advertising artificial, as they did not feel their lives had anything to do with American college life. A new creative brief was therefore developed focusing on *Being Real* for the UK market.

Using video diaries, the advertising agency developed new scripts that incorporated insights from real conversations in British universities. Three scripts were chosen which worked very well in research and were made into TV ads known as the *Real Students* campaign. Immediately following the airing of *Real Students*, Bright White experienced the largest single increase in sales ever achieved in a quarterly period. By the end of the year, Bright White had met its objective of becoming the leading brand and the most popular brand amongst young consumers.

Evidence that the success of Bright White was due to the *Real Students* campaign included increased advertising awareness in relation to other brands. Research showed that young people were enthusiastic about Bright White and thought it was true to their lives and attitudes. The success was not due to other factors. Domos did not introduce a price cut, new product launches, reformulations, changes in packaging or distribution, or increase advertising spend. Other factors such as an increase in the population or increases in disposable income could also be eliminated. If these had been significant, they would have affected the total market.

The brand was not on track to meet its objectives before the *Real Students* campaign. This was dramatically reversed by maintaining the theme of a global advertising idea but adapting the American advertisements to ones based on insights from British consumers. Furthermore, Domos successfully rolled out the brand in 14 countries across Europe and Asia, with advertising that similarly recognised each country's local needs.

2. Find a TVC (Television Commercial) for a shampoo or other hair product. This commercial is going to be aired in the Republic of Terra Firma. Research reveals the following legislation regarding television advertising in the Republic of Terra Firma:

- Comparative advertising is forbidden
- A person cannot be shown using their left hand
- Women must be shown with feminine dignity
- A woman's body must be completely covered; only the hands can be shown uncovered
- A woman can be filmed from the back of the head only when advertising a facial or hair product
- Religious symbols or pictures of any kind are forbidden.

Suggest adaptations to the commercial for the market of Terra Firma.

3. Devise a marketing communications strategy and media strategy for CleanIT! in the Republic of Terra Firma, and present your strategies to Domos. Read the information below to help you plan your presentation.

Domos is planning to introduce CleanIT! to the Republic of Terra Firma. As Domos' agency, your research has uncovered the following information about the Republic:

- Great Britain colonised the country, and Terra Firma became an independent republic in 1951.
- The Republic of Terra Firma is currently a member of the Commonwealth of Nations.
- The population of the Republic of Terra Firma is approximately 75 million.
- 20% of the population live in the capital city of Capitale.
- The official language of government and the civil service is English, and there are 5 different native languages spoken in the country.
- 30% of the population is illiterate, and women are three times more likely to be illiterate than men.
- Everyone has access to the main electricity supply.
- Faster broadband speeds only exist in Capitale.
- There are approximately 35 million TV sets in the country, but projected TV screens exist in many rural communities.
- There are three state analogue terrestrial TV channels; 60% of content is broadcast in English.
- International satellite TV channels have gained a foothold in Capitale.
- Radio is popular, with the largest percentage of the population tuning into sports coverage.
- Billboards are prolific. Posters are colourful and busy, with all the space covered by images.
- Cinema is incredibly popular.
- There is one national newspaper, *Terra Firma News* printed in English, but it tends to reflect government opinion.
- There are three additional regional newspapers.
- Access to international press is only available in Capitale.
- Cricket, rugby and tennis are national sports, and the best players become national heroes.
- There are no women's national teams for any sport.
- Due to low literacy rates, pictures on packaging often explain the product and its use.

Present your strategies to Domos.

D Structure of the Global Marketing Communications Industry

1. Match the name of the type of agency (1-8) to the correct description (a-h):

1. digital agency
2. house/in-house agency/communications function
3. boutique / creative boutique agency
4. holding company
5. brand agency
6. full-service agency
7. advertising agency
8. public relations agency

a. ____ An agency that conceives and creates mass media marketing concepts, often specialising in ATL marketing. Digital marketing has changed and is changing this kind of agency so that it increasingly offers BTL activities.

b. ____ An agency that handles website design, mobile applications, e-mail marketing, search engine optimisation (SEO), e-commerce, and/or social media.

MARKETING COMMUNICATIONS IN ENGLISH

c. ____ An agency that focuses on developing brand and corporate identity.

d. ____ An agency owned and operated by the advertiser itself, which can range in size from a single communications or advertising manager to a department to an independent entity within the organisation.

e. ____ An agency that handles all aspects of marketing communications campaigns including research, planning, design, production, and placement. This can also include public relations, sales promotion, direct marketing, and marketing strategy.

f. ____ An agency that provides a limited service, such as one that does creative work but does not provide media planning, research, and so on. This usually refers to a relatively small company.

g. ____ A group that controls a huge number of different agency brands worldwide which generally doesn't involve itself in day-to-day marketing but works to encourage intra-group synergy and development of strategy. The largest global groups are sometimes known as the "big four". Acquisition frequently changes numbers, and the current big players can be checked online.

h. ____ An agency that creates positive relations between an organisation and its publics.

2. You are going to give a presentation about a real-world advertising agency. Choose an agency, of any type, that exists on the market today. Research these areas:

- Type of agency and any network or holding company the agency belongs to
- History of the agency
- Manpower behind the success of the agency
- The agency's main clients
- The agency's work/best advertisements

Present your findings to the class.

E Job Application

1. Read this job advertisement and the following job application.

Global Marketing Communications Manager at Domos

Our goal is consistent global communications and we are seeking to employ a global marketing communications manager to help us achieve this. The successful candidate will have a proven track record creating successful PR and advertising campaigns, and communicating effectively across all digital channels to attract and retain customers.

The role involves:
- designing and creating communications for all marketing channels
- planning and executing the company's participation in global promotional events and trade shows
- building and developing relationships with stakeholders and media
- working collaboratively with managers to implement marketing plans
- providing feedback to the company on market requirements, current industry trends and challenges
- managing projects and communications to budget and meeting deadlines.

The ideal candidate has:
- a background in journalism, content, or copywriting
- experience living and working abroad

- fluency in English plus at least one other language
- excellent written and verbal communication skills
- a minimum of a bachelor's degree, preferably in journalism, marketing or communications
- experience in global communications
- knowledge of social media channels
- experience with project management

This job suits a self-starter who pays meticulous attention to detail. Applicants should be confident and mature with drive, energy, and the ability to work independently.

If you match our requirements, send your application to Ned J. Smith, Human Resources, at Domos Headquarters, Domos Way, Middletown, United Kingdom explaining fully why you should be put on the shortlist for interview.

---

31 July 20xx

Dear Mr Smith,

Further to your job advertisement published on the "Marketing Today" website, I am applying for the post of Global Marketing Communications Manager at Domos.

My bachelor's and master's degree in marketing and sales communications combined with my practical international experience working as an assistant corporate communications manager and communications manager in multinational companies make me an ideal candidate. My track record in developing and implementing communication strategies on a global scale is proven, and I have successfully developed international media relations and contacts. Moreover, I speak and write English fluently and have studied in both the United States and the United Kingdom, completing my master's thesis in English.

The position at Domos represents the challenge I am seeking and would enable me to take my career to the next level whilst working for a global company with dynamic brands. I am available for a personal interview at a time and place that is convenient for you, and look forward to hearing from you.

Yours faithfully,
Sabine J. Mustermann

CURRICULUM VITAE

Name: Sabine J. Mustermann
Nationality: German
Address: Blindweg 52, 12252 Berlin, Germany
Telephone: +49 30 222 555
Mobile: +49 122 555 222
Email: sjmustermann@email.com

Education
1995-2003
Republik Gymnasium, Kleinstadt, Germany (grammar/high school)
German Abitur (A levels/high school graduation)

2003-2007
University of Grossstadt, Germany
B.A. Marketing Communications Management
Including 2005-2006 study year abroad at Harvard University, USA.

2007-2008
University of Middletown, U.K.
M.A. Marketing and Sales Communications
Thesis: Social Media Management

Experience
2011-present
Schwester und Schwester GmbH, Berlin, Germany
Communications Manager
• Development and implementation of communication strategies to reach target audiences
• Creating and implementing an international corporate identity
• Editing global company websites and communications
• Negotiation of event vendor contracts
• Design of promotional material worldwide
• Introduction of internal communications, including a global in-house newsletter
• Liaison with worldwide subsidiaries

2008-2011
Bruder und Bruder GmbH, Berlin, Germany
Assistant Corporate Communications Manager
• Implementation of communication strategies
• Development of company website and social media content
• Tracking of international media content
• Establishing relations with media
• Support of sales and marketing activities

Languages
German: mother tongue
English: C1 level
Mandarin Chinese: B1 level

2. With a partner, assess whether Sabine Mustermann should be shortlisted for a job interview with Domos by listing both the positive and negative aspects of her application.

positive	negative

overall assessment:

WORD BANK: GLOBAL MARKETING COMMUNICATION

ethnocentric orientation: Orientation towards the home country; an unconscious belief that the home country approach to business is superior.

geocentric orientation: Orientation based upon the assumption that there are similarities and differences between countries that can be understood and recognised in an integrated world strategy.

polycentric orientation: believing that it is necessary to adapt to local culture and practice.

ANSWER KEY

Chapter 1: Branding

A.

1. h	3. f	5. i	7. c	9. e
2. a	4. j	6. g	8. d	10. b

B.

1.

a. "concrete" = tangible, "emotional" = intangible.

b. CONCRETE - name, logo, graphics, packaging, symbols, colours, sounds, design, mission statement EMOTIONAL - image, promise, personality, the "story", perception, connection, the "essence", a mental picture, culture, the "soul", (strong, positive) associations, memories, essential truth.
There can be an overlap. For example, an airline can promise comfort which is tangible but can provoke emotion.

3.

a. "trademark", provides consumers with a reason to / the motivation to choose / buy / recommend, provides brand experience and delivers on promises.

4.

b. breaking through message clutter, building a relationship, providing a clear message, being credible, creating loyalty, being consistent.

D.

2.

define / position / support / care / nurture / maintain / develop the brand, build brand awareness, build loyal customers, develop strategic plans, implement marketing and communication plans, maintain brand equity, increase brand value, increase sales, understand the competition.

E.

1.

a. private label	d. distinctive	g. (brand) spokesperson
b. new entrants	e. to (re)position	h. to roll out
c. brand extensions	f. heritage brand	i. to unveil
		j. to air

2.

Positioning is a marketing strategy that aims to make a brand occupy a distinct position, relative to competing brands, in the mind of the target market. This can involve emphasising distinguishing features and benefits and creating image. The target market can be determined by demographic, psychographic (lifestyle) and/or geographic variables.

    a) In the 1950s, the target market was stay at home married women (housewives) with children. Thepositioning was reliability, trustworthiness and daily efficiency and strength compared to competitors' products.

    b) In the 1990s, the target market was younger people of both genders. The positioning was based on tradition, trustworthiness, heritage and the home. The repositioning may not have worked as the younger target did not feel addressed as regards changes in lifestyle, wants and needs.

c) In the 21st century, the target market was both genders, catering for changes in lifestyle as re gards time spent in the home and cleaning the home. The positioning was care, intelligent, environmentally-friendly but efficient.

F.

1.

Story telling has a long tradition in human history and is a fundamental human activity to share and transfer information and knowledge. We are told stories from a very young age (story at bedtime) so that story telling can be comforting. Stories put information into a context that we can relate to and we relate stories to our own experience so that narratives make sense of the world. Story telling can cross culture capturing the essence of social interaction and human action. Stories tap into emotions and create a relaxed state whereas cognitive overload creates a state of stress. They can be fundamental for meaning and memory, motivating, engaging and entertaining and create a scenario where we want to know the end result.

Different areas in our brains are activated when experiencing the events of a story.
- a brand story can be told through advertising, journalism & PR, traditional media, social media, crowd-sourced content, interactive media, new technologies (e.g. virtual reality).
- good brand stories are based on authenticity, reality, a good product, creativity.
- a brand story can change consumers' perceptions, bring values and mission to life, create credibility, differentiate and set the brand apart from the competition, create brand loyalty and brand advocates, develop repeat sales and a foundation for future growth.

G.

1.

Characteristics of an effective brand spokesperson:
Likeability; credibility; trustworthiness; charisma; authenticity; physical attractiveness; memorable, identification with target consumer as regards beliefs, attitudes, preferences, behaviour(s) / association with the product (sports); personality; expertise; presents him or herself well; commanding presence, a lack of negative publicity; sports – not linked to one team.

Chapter 2: Campaign Management

A.

1.

1. h	3. i	5. b	7. g	9. c
2. a	4. j	6. e	8. f	10. d

B.

1.

The brief gives all the pertinent information in a written form giving everyone involved a campaign the same information and a platform to kick off a project or creative work. It can be discussed and/ or negotiated. This puts everyone on the same page and the document can be consulted at any time in the process. It clarifies expectations, definitions, objectives etc. and helps to keep everyone on track.

2.

a. Product Manager, pm@domos.co.uk

b. TV: 30 second commercial clips – (national with roll-out to 10 European countries). Billboard Advertising. Print. Point of Sale (POS).

c. There have been 4 major players in the household cleaning sector with more or less equal market shares for approximately 25 years

d. Research and Development Environmental Report

e. Children, teenagers and parents should view Mr Super Clean as loveable, funky and cool so that theywill purchase future Mr Super Clean merchandising

f. core target market: males and females from the ages of 8 to 15 and their parents

g. cleanliness is vital but concerns, feelings of guilt about using cleaning products

h. reasons to believe

i. statements under "what consumers told us"

j. everything under mandatory

k. loveable, funky, cool, caring

l. review revised creative, final full creative & media presentation

m. consumer benefit

C.

1.
   a. comparative
   b. functional
   c. generic
   d. pre-emptive
   e. emotional

2.
   a. Rational
   b. Humour
   c. Fear
   d. Music
   e. Sex
   f. Bandwagon
   g. Emotion
   h. Scarcity

3.
   1. g
   2. b
   3. ih. Scarcity
   4. d
   5. f
   6. h7. c
   8. e
   9. a

D.

1.
   1. Background
   2. Application
   3. Elements
   4. Presentation
   5. Scheduling
   6. Shooting

2.
   a. reaction shot
   b. very wide shot
   c. POV
   d. two-shot
   e. over the shoulder shot
   f. extreme close up
   g. close up
   h. medium close up
   i. wide shot
   j. mid-shot/medium shot

3.
   a. bird's eye angle
   b. eye level angle
   c. low angle
   d. high angle
   e. Dutch angle

4.
   1. b
   2. d
   3. e
   4. c
   5. f
   6. a

G.

1.

1. g	4. j	7. b	10. m	13. e
2. n	5. k	8. l	11. i	14. h
3. d	6. f	9. a	12. c	

Chapter 3: Below the Line

A.

1.

ATL: print, broad reach, image, radio, category leader, macro, branding, outdoor, awareness, TV, conventional, gross ratings.

BTL: sampling, events, impulse purchasing, insights into ROI, measurable, quantifiable, POS, direct mail, targeted, cost-effective, followers, personal, PR, specific, engagement, likes, direct mail, challenger brand, micro, trackable. Depending on the brand (challenger brand) – image, branding.

TTL: blurring of the line, integrated communication, consistency, multiple points.

B.

1.

a. Triggered email is sent in response to the consumer's behaviour: unsubscribing to a newsletter, working out at the gym and reaching a training goal etc.

b. Abandoned cart email is sent when the consumer starts the online buying process but does not complete the purchase.

c. Timing and relevance – i.e. right content at the right time, state of the art software and up to date technology, personalisation.

C.

1.

1. So, What Are Press Releases?
2. Make Sure It's Newsworthy
3. The Beginning
4. Style
5. 'Inverted Pyramid'
6. Shorter is Sweeter
7. Avoid Specialist Language
8. Include Quotations
9. The Last Paragraph
10. Check It

D.

2.

c. cultural events, product launch, press conference, corporate party, road show, award ceremony, film premiere, fashion show, Olympics, soccer World Cup.

d. knowledge of project management, identify target audience, identify brand personality, devise an event concept, plan logistics.

e. participation, engagement.

f. choice of site, cash flow, procurement, scheduling, site design, technology, health and safety, first-aid, environment, crowd management, logistics, sound, light, video, security, catering (depending on type of event)

g. evaluate ROI, get feedback, record feedback, review event, close project.

Chapter 4: Promotion

A.

a. 3	c. 8	e. 6	g. 4
b. 1	d. 7	f. 2	h. 5

B.

1.

a. 5	c. 2	e. 1
b. 4	d. 6	f. 3

2.

a.
a. to pester
b. cold calling

b.
a. to opt in
b. affinity
c. giveaway, free sample
d. footfall
e. integrated marketing communications campaign

c.
a. BOGOF
b. prospect

d.
a. gimmick
b. upselling

e.
a. spam, junk
b. perpetuate

f.
a. to opt out
b. breach

C.

1.

The following aspects can be considered in comparing the 4 promotions and answering the questions at the end of each:

- promotion objectives
- suitability of the promotion for the product / brand
- lack of insurance for worst case scenario
- originality of promotion
- wording, length, and scope of the promotion
- the year the promotion was run (i.e. before or after internet and social media)
- internal management controls: assessment of worst case scenario
- internal management response
- role of the PR department
- consumer perception(s)
- the size of the company

E.

3.

1. essential	4. differentiate	7. mirror	10. strategic	13. attached to
2. enhance	5. purpose	8. subliminal	11. appropriate	14. effectiveness
3. distinguish	6. target market	messages	12. subjective	15. amendments
		9. inappropriate		

5.

Physical: handling, protection, distinctiveness, information, convenience, manifestation of brand, instruction.

Psychological: authenticity, trust, grabbing attention, reflecting brand personality, emotion, motivation, symbolism, signifying value.

Chapter 5: Guerrilla Marketing

A.

1.

1. g	4. e	7. f
2. b	5. a	8. d
3. h	6. c	

2.

a. influencer marketing

b. wild posting

c. street marketing

d. viral marketing

e. projection advertising

f. ambient advertising

g. stealth marketing

h. ambush marketing

B.

1.

a. fierce rivalry

b. brand that is not a category leader

c. product that embodies interests and attitudes, giving consumers a means of self-expression

d. being aware of brands rather than products, purchasing brands due to image and perception

e. recommendations to and conversations with other prospective customers

f. sense of excitement and interest regenerated by media coverage

2.

Tone™ was a challenger brand and guerrilla marketing fits challenger brands better than category leaders. Guerrilla marketing suited the brand personality and felt authentic; the campaign was cohesive and the owners of the brand were comfortable taking a risk.

Chapter 6: Corporate Identity and Corporate Image

A.

1.

elements of CI: Name, logo, colours, typeface, typography, imagery, tone and voice.
aims: Coherence, differentiation, reflection of aims and values, representation.
protection: copyright protection, correctness and consistency.

B.

2.

Constant actions: Corporate advertising, sponsorship, linking with charities or non-profit organisations, social media management.
Reasons for change: Crisis can come from almost anywhere - online examples show how diverse problems are. Image can be damaged because the company has got or done something wrong but also because of false accusations or being misunderstood.
Action for repair: good crisis management

D.

2.

"Domos Tablets" - The problem was unforeseen. Domos reacted quickly, did not let the problem escalate, prevented media backlash and protected public safety. The action was decisive, transparent and honest and Domos acted correctly by admitting the mistake, apologising and rectifying the problem. The offer of the voucher might be seen as overreaction but proved to be the correct action in the long-term. The company was willing to lose money in the short-term for long-term benefits.

"Giant Burger Firing" - Giant Burger was inconsistent, defensive and argumentative. It failed to contain the crisis or address concerns and actually hid criticism. Instead of reacting and taking positive action, the company escalated the situation amplifying negative PR. The company needed more professional social media management.

Chapter 7: Marketing Research

A.

1.

Primary Research: Original, current, verified, unique, survey, questionnaire, observation, interview.
Secondary Research: Desk, internet, websites, blogs, government reports, newspapers, company accounts.

3.

a. Secondary research
b. Primary research
c. Secondary research
d. Primary research

e. Primary research
f. Secondary research
g. Primary research

h. Secondary research
i. Secondary research
j. Primary research

B.

2.

a. quantitative
b. ethnographic
c. quantitative

d. ethnographic
e. qualitative
f. quantitative

g. qualitative
h. quantitative
i. ethnographic
j. qualitative

C.

2.

Closed-ended: Multiple choice, check box, quantifiable, percentages, drop down box, demographic information, conclusive, ranking

Open-ended: Unanticipated answer, unique answer, freedom and space, exploratory, qualitative, in-depth, unlimited response, complex explanation necessary, consumer behaviour information.

3.

a. Open-ended question
b. Closed-ended question
c. Closed-ended question
d. Open-ended question
e. Open-ended question
f. Closed-ended question
g. Open-ended question

h. Closed-ended question
i. Closed-ended question
j. Closed-ended question
k. Open-ended question
l. Closed-ended question
m. Open-ended question
n. Closed-ended question

o. Closed-ended question
p. Open-ended question
q. Closed-ended question
r. Open-ended question
s. Open-ended question
t. Closed-ended question

E.

1.

1. c
2. e

3. f
4. a

5. d
6. b

2.

a. research objectives
b. research tools
c. interviewer bias

d. resonate with prospects
e. consumer insights
f. elicit responses

g. brand advocates
h. time to market
i. gut instinct

Chapter 8: Global Marketing Communications
Introduction

1.

a. An international company probably exports. Communications will often reflect culture and values of the home nation of the headquarters. A multinational operates in a number of overseas markets using agents, distributors and maybe establishing subsidiaries. The marketing mix is adapted to overseas operations and the focus switches to a polycentric approach and adaption with orientation on the home nation. A global organisation sells common products worldwide. Communications recognise that markets consist of similarities and differences and orientate to geocentrism with a world market strategy.

b. research, business practices, language, culture, local tastes and preferences, politics, currency, legal framework, competition, cultural icons and symbols, customs, religion, dress, food, geography, infrastructure, level of technology, brand status, managing at a geographical distance.

c. whether to standardise (same product and communications worldwide) or adapt (to local taste and preference), consistency of messages and communication, language, translation, whether name - slogans - claims work outside the home market.

g. in common: Good global campaign management, consistency of message and communications (within constraints of the local market), brand status, quality of product and service, tapping into basic human needs and emotions.

product categories: Consumer durables, electronics, fashion, luxury goods and perfume can most likely be sold throughout all markets. Consumer non-durables, including food products, are more sensitive to differences in national tastes and habits making them more likely to need changes for various markets.

h. Global holding companies and worldwide networks in the communications industry tend to the global trend of adopting English as a working language of the company. Agency clients may also have adopted English as their main working language of business. So, an agency in France may work for the national company of a global client presenting campaigns for the French market but do this in English, for example. Marketing communications for that national company may have to reflect French language and culture even though the business itself is conducted in English. So, English can be seen as a global marketing language/tool with names, slogans etc. in English and/or a business tool to successfully conduct the business of marketing communications.

Many expressions in the industry have their root in native speaker (USA and UK) culture and the English language. Moreover, online content is overwhelmingly in English with statistics showing English at over 50% to 80% of content. Other languages are at around 6% and lower. The English language therefore has to be a major factor if content marketing, digital marketing and social media are playing an increasingly significant role.

Taking current trends, popular culture, the rapid drive to English as the global language (particularly of business) and the globalisation of the marketing industry as factors, it can be concluded that English is the language of global marketing communications. On the other hand, it can be argued that global marketing communications will always need local adaptation.

i. Many examples of bad and ineffective translations of advertising slogans and marketing messages exist online. These invariably have a negative impact on sales and brand status. Greater investment in professional translating and checking with nationals on the target market at an earlier stage would actually save money in the longer term.

A.

2.

a. in computer, internet technology, online services - technology is playing a much more significant role.

b. perceptions and attitudes towards what constitutes unhealthy and healthy food and drink, perceptions and attitudes towards tobacco products, a tendency to consume entertainment in the home, maybe environmental concerns about vehicles.

c. Japan and South Korea. These countries have become successful in developing global brands and overcoming past difficulties such as the devastation of war, attitudes towards and perception of "Made in Japan" or "Made in Korea" as well as a reliance on overseas aid. South Korea is now a technologically advanced country. Time and brand management appear to be factors. Modern marketing and branding may have their roots in the U.S.A. but there are open questions as to whether other countries are catching up and to what extent this is happening and will happen. Additionally, business expands by acquisition and the significance of considering nationality in a global marketplace can also be questioned.

d. There could be a variety of reasons, e.g. a failure to keep up with technological changes, a failure to adapt to changing consumer attitudes and perceptions or some other kind of crisis or damage to the brand.

3.

c. China may lack the education and culture of creativity needed for global branding but has the potential to buy talent and/or brands. The power of Chinese (or indeed other nations') brands may increase, especially if taking the experience of Japan and South Korea into consideration. Further considerations could be (unforeseen) technological change, political change or changes in consumer attitudes and lifestyle and the impact of globalisation in defining brands according to nationality.

d. It is possible there is little overlap in the two lists and there are a number of companies that are not household names in the companies' list. These might be companies in sectors such as banking or the oil industry which are not generally known. China has some of the world's largest companies and/or brands that are huge in China but not yet the biggest global brands. The U.S.A. is still dominant in terms of branding.

B.

1.

a. Standardisation	e. Standardisation	i. Adaption
b. Adaption	f. Adaption	j. Standardisation
c. Standardisation	g. Standardisation	k. Adaption
d. Adaption	h. Adaption	l. Standardisation

C.

1.

a. Young people buy on recommendation from peers not parents.

b. Both countries have the same language. The British consume American media and culture and would understand American college life.

c. Young people did not connect with the brand, the advertising message and stories of American college life and competition was a threat to positioning.

d. Increased sales, increased advertising awareness, customers stated they connected to Bright White, Domos did not change anything else in the marketing mix - only the advertising campaign, the rest of the category did not increase sales, the campaign adaptation was successfully rolled out to other countries.

D.

1.

a. 7   d. 2   g. 4
b. 1   e. 6   h. 8
c. 5   f. 3

www.ingramcontent.com/pod-product-compliance
Lightning Source LLC
Chambersburg PA
CBHW080522110426
42742CB00017B/3200